Letting Go of Ed

A Guide to Recovering from Your Eating Disorder

Letting Go of Ed

A Guide to Recovering
from Your Eating Disorder

Pippa Wilson

BOOKS

Winchester, UK
Washington, USA

First published by O-Books, 2011
O-Books is an imprint of John Hunt Publishing Ltd., Laurel House, Station Approach,
Alresford, Hants, SO24 9JH, UK
office1@o-books.net
www.o-books.com

For distributor details and how to order please visit the 'Ordering' section on our website.

ISBN: 978 1 84694 698 1

A CIP catalogue record for this book is available from the British Library.

Design: Stuart Davies

Printed in the UK by CPI Antony Rowe
Printed in the USA by Offset Paperback Mfrs, Inc

We operate a distinctive and ethical publishing philosophy in all
areas of our business, from our global network of authors to
production and worldwide distribution.

CONTENTS

For the Wilson women,
past, present and future

Acknowledgements

Thank you to Ally, for his patience and support; to Anna, for her wisdom and guidance; to Laura, for her faith and fairy-godmothering; to Tracy, for her enthusiasm and belief; to Emily, for her humor and spirit; to Emma, for her encouragement and ideas; and to George, for simply being.

Introduction

Before we get into the nitty-gritty of eating disorders and letting go of yours, you probably have some questions about this book.

What's this book about?

This is not a book about your eating disorder. This is a book about you.

If you're looking for a book crammed full of psychobabble and medical jargon that drones on about the technicalities of eating disorders, this isn't it. If you want to read a gory horror story of anorexia and bulimia, a tragic account of abuse or an angry rant about a lost childhood, look elsewhere. And if you're seeking a book that lays down rules for how to recover, complete with details about food, calories, weight and exercise, don't bother reading any further.

This book doesn't focus on your eating disorder, because that's a complete waste of time. Your eating disorder isn't the problem, it's the symptom. This book, therefore, won't arm you for battle with your eating disorder. Recovery isn't about waging war and emerging victorious. Recovery is about focusing on all the other areas of your life that need healing so that you don't need your eating disorder anymore. And then it just slips quietly, simply, beautifully away from you: no battle, no struggle, no I-fought-Ed-and-won bumper sticker.

In this book you won't find a magic cure for your eating disorder. But what you will find are information, ideas and support to help you heal from the pain inside and build a happier relationship with yourself. Then and only then can you let go of your eating problems.

Who's this book for?

Quite simply, this book is for anyone who's unhappy in their eating and body image irrespective of sex, age, race, occupation or belief system.

You may be diagnosed with an eating disorder, or you may not. You may be lost in a world of anorexia, bulimia or binge eating, or you may be a perpetual dieter who just can't find a happy place when it comes to food. Whatever the scale of your eating distress, this book can help you find a way to let go.

This book speaks directly to those who are struggling with an eating disorder, but it will also help anyone who wants to learn more about eating disorders: what causes them, how they work and the kinds of things you need to address in order to recover. You may be a loved one or friend of someone who's struggling with their eating. From the outside, it can be very difficult to understand eating disorders and why someone would develop one. This book opens the door to the strange world of illness and unhappiness that surrounds Ed, and equips you with understanding that can make a real difference in how you support someone in their recovery.

Who's Ed?

Throughout this book I refer to your eating disorder, in whatever form it takes, as Ed.

Partly, I do this because it makes recovery a little less clinical and a little more light-hearted: the very words "eating disorder" can make you feel depressed and hopeless.

But I also believe that personifying Ed can be a helpful strategy when working on letting go of your eating disorder. By imagining Ed as a living, breathing entity that forms a part of you, you can really work on your relationship with this aspect of yourself. Believe me, it's liberating to stand in a supermarket, struggling with your thoughts, and say out loud, "Oh shove off, Ed, you nutter."

Ed was my name for my eating disorder. It doesn't matter what name you choose. Perhaps you prefer Anna for anorexia or

Bill for bulimia. Just do what feels right.

How do I work through this book?

However you like. Very few readers will start on page one and be guided through the book to recovery by the final page. You're likely to dip in and out of the book; to read sections and then come back to them at later stages. You may also decide some sections don't apply to you, and so skip them altogether. That's fine.

The key to reading this book (and any other self-development material) is to trust that you will take from the writing exactly what you need at the time of reading. If you aren't ready to take on a concept or follow a suggestion, you won't. But the idea may remain at the back of your mind, and when the time's right you can begin to explore it.

So follow your instincts, and read this book however you like, over whatever time span suits you. There are no rules, only what works for you.

Why did you write this book?

Everything you'll read on these pages is born of my own journey to recover from Ed. When it comes to eating disorders, sadly I've been there, done that, got the T-shirt. A childhood marred by abuse and bereavement drove me straight into Ed's arms, and I spent many long, dark years dancing between binge eating, bulimia and anorexia.

And then I gave it all up. I let go of Ed and took hold of life.

The road to recovery was hard, damn hard. It was agonizing, exhausting, terrifying. But I look back now and am so glad that I kept going. Nothing beats life after Ed: the sense of quiet and calm inside; the connection with the world; the freedom to be the true you; the ability to feel, really feel; the sheer bliss of being safe and at ease in your own skin.

The author Toni Morrison once said, "If there's a book you

really want to read but it hasn't been written yet, then you must write it." Well, here it is: the book I wish I could have read while I was lost in Ed's world.

I hope you will find comfort, understanding and inspiration in these pages and, above all, the conviction that you really *can* let go of your eating disorder and be free at last.

Understanding eating disorders

In recent years public awareness of eating disorders has greatly increased. Thanks to media hype and the sheer prevalence of Ed, these days just about everyone recognizes the term "eating disorder" and has a rough idea of what it means. But therein lies the problem: these rough ideas are often rather muddled and inaccurate. So let's start with the basics. What exactly is an eating disorder?

Relating (to) the story of Ed

Move over Cinderella, there's a new fairy tale in town: the story of Ed...

Once upon a time there was a girl who was going through a really tough time. She was angry, scared, lonely, sad and hurt. She needed someone, something, anything to help her, to rescue her, to take away the pain and make her feel safer, calmer. But the girl was all alone: she was sure that no one saw her pain, no one understood, no one could help her. She became desperate; she just couldn't cope. She didn't know what to do, where to turn.

But then, one day, the girl met Ed. Ed was exciting and new. Ed seemed to care about her and want to help. Quickly, the girl and Ed became firm friends.

In some ways, Ed was good to the girl. Ed was faithful, loyal and consistent. Ed was there for the girl whenever she felt sad, lonely, angry or lost. Ed was reassuring and calming. Ed helped the girl cope with her feelings and made the pain more bearable. Ed made the girl feel wonderfully empty and numb.

But the girl soon discovered that Ed had a dark side. Ed could be cruel, manipulative, controlling and domineering. Ed was uncaring, destructive, hurtful and poisonous. Ed was possessive and jealous, and held on tightly. Ed made the girl feel desperate, lonely and ill. Ed was not edifying company.

The girl developed a love-hate relationship with Ed. She loved Ed, but hated Ed; needed Ed, but wanted to get away from Ed.

As time went on, the girl became more and more unhappy having Ed in her life. She began to argue with Ed and struggle to break free from the friendship, but she kept finding herself drawn back into Ed's welcoming embrace. Ed and the girl went round and round in dizzying circles, dancing a fiery tango, pulling away and then moving intimately close. Although the girl wanted to let go, she just couldn't seem to get out of Ed's clutches.

The girl's friend had become her foe.

This was my story, and yours is no doubt similar. Ed is your friend, your confidante, your savior and, ultimately, your enemy.

Seeing how eating disorders work

So how do you get sucked into the world of Ed? Well, eating disorders follow the same pattern...

1. You struggle with your feelings. You may be very angry, scared or sad. Your feelings overwhelm you and you desperately need to find a way to cope. You feel isolated and frustrated that you can't control how you're feeling. You feel angry with your feelings and with yourself for not managing them better. You just want these feelings to disappear.

2. You want to get control. Inside your body are all these horrible feelings that you can't control. When you look in the mirror these feelings manifest in your reflection. You hate the way you look. You feel ugly, fat, unlovable. You think that if you could just control your body, you'd feel better inside. You start to fantasize about being thinner, fitter, more toned.

3. You start off with "normal" changes. You may weigh yourself more often, make weight-loss plans and go on a diet. You start small, with little changes that are okay to the outside

world. You find you enjoy your new direction.

4. You take your first step across the line. You decide to take things to the next level. Tentatively, you try out a behavior that you know isn't entirely healthy. You may start skipping meals, eating less and less or more and more, pushing your body harder at the gym, taking laxatives or vomiting. Soon, this new behavior becomes the norm: something you feel comfortable doing.

5. You add on more and more behaviors. You like the powerful feeling your behavior gives you; the sense of control and mastery over your body; the distraction the behavior provides from your feelings. You feel like you've found the magic answer, the way to numb those horrid feelings. You move faster and faster into the eating disorder, trying new behaviors, seeing how far you can take your mind, your body. You push the boundaries. How long can you go without food? How many chips can you eat in one sitting? How often can you vomit? How many miles can you do on the treadmill?

6. The worm turns: you can't stop. You're addicted to your eating disorder. Although you still like how Ed distances you from your feelings, you're feeling ill and exhausted, and people are starting to notice, and perhaps even interfere. You try to step back again, to lessen or even stop the behaviors, but you find you're trapped. You can't seem to control Ed: it has a mind of its own. You start to feel scared.

7. You go round and round in circles. You get stuck in a vicious circle:

- You do something "bad" like binging, vomiting or starving.
- You beat yourself up for your "bad" behavior and hate yourself even more. You tell yourself you'll stop now, you won't do it again, this was the last time.
- You start to feel scary emotions like sadness, anxiety and rage, and the feelings are overwhelming. You desperately

need the pressure to lift, the chaos to calm.

- You give into the mounting pressure and resort to Ed. You may starve, or exercise for hours, or binge and purge. For a little while, you get blessed relief. You feel calmer, empty, numb.
- But then you beat yourself up for your "bad" behavior and hate yourself even more. You tell yourself you'll stop now, you won't do it again, this was the last time...

And so the cycle continues, day in, day out, in an exhausting, dizzying cyclone. Until, that is, you start to confront the feelings you're avoiding. Then, and only then, does the spinning slow, the vicious circle break.

Recognizing eating disorder symptoms

An eating disorder is usually a combination of acting in abnormal ways around eating and thinking and feeling negatively about food and your body.

Here are some eating disorder behaviors:

- Bingeing: eating large quantities of food in a short period of time
- Categorizing foods as "good", "bad", "safe" and "naughty"
- Chewing food and spitting it out without swallowing
- Counting calories
- Cutting food into tiny pieces
- Eating privately and secretly
- Exercising to extremes
- Having rituals for food: that certain foods can't touch, for example
- Lying about your food intake and behavior
- Purging: making yourself sick
- Refusing to eat a lot of foods (fussy eating)

- Setting rules for food and eating: for example, "I can't eat after 6pm" or "I can only eat 500 calories a day"
- Taking laxatives often and in increasingly high doses
- Weighing yourself obsessively

Here are some things you may feel:

- Ashamed of your body
- Drawn to food, like it calls to you
- Frightened of food and eating
- Naughty/guilty when you eat
- Out of control around food; that food has power
- Panicky in food-related environments like supermarkets and restaurants
- Repulsed by others' eating
- Sickened by the sensation of eating or having a full stomach
- Terrified of gaining weight
- Uncomfortable in your body

You may have one, two, a few, many or all of the symptoms on these lists, and others besides.

Understanding that Ed is really about how you feel

When you have an eating disorder, it's tempting to focus on your behaviors. After all, they're destructive and dangerous. However, how you *feel* is a much better indicator of whether you have an eating disorder and, if so, how bad it is.

Ed is a state of mind, a way you think and feel. Sometimes you may act on your thoughts and feelings, but this isn't always the case. You may have an eating disorder but none of the telltale behaviors.

For example, for several months during my illness I was able to control my behaviors. Friends and family thought I was recovering (or even recovered) because I stopped starving, binging and purging, and even gained a little weight. But inside I was no better at all. I still desperately wanted to starve and binge, but I was bullying myself into eating "normally." Although I may have seemed better on the outside, inside I was still just as scared and anxious about food, eating, my weight and my body. I exhibited none of the behaviors associated with Ed but I still very much had an eating disorder, and it wasn't long before Ed took control once more.

On the other hand, some people may *act* like they have an eating disorder, but be perfectly healthy. For example, my friend Karen has some eating habits that a nutritionist may not deem normal. She never eats breakfast, has a small snack for lunch and then eats a lot in the evening. She's a vegetarian who pretty much lives on fruit, veg, rice, pasta, eggs, cheese, soya milk and yoghurt. She's also pretty slim and she does a lot of exercise: swimming, cycling, running and so on. Karen exhibits some behaviors that you may associate with an eating disorder, but she doesn't have one at all. Why? Because Karen is happy. She doesn't feel scared or anxious about her eating; in fact, she doesn't think much at all about food. She doesn't use food as a way to deal with her feelings; nor does she feel out of control around food. She enjoys what she eats and feels she eats according to her hunger. She likes her body, but she doesn't force it to stay slim. She simply enjoys exercising.

Ed, then, is all about feelings. So true recovery from Ed isn't about gaining or losing weight, eating more "normally" or giving up binging and purging. True recovery is about how you feel inside. When you let go of Ed, you feel calmer, more accepting of yourself and your body, and much happier around food. And feeling better makes the behaviors better.

In a nutshell: feelings are primary; behaviors are secondary.

Categorizing eating disorders

People often categorize eating disorders into three types: anorexia, bulimia and binge eating disorder. Put simply, if you have anorexia your predominant behavior is self-starvation; if you have bulimia you binge and purge regularly; and if you have binge eating disorder you binge but do not purge.

All too often, medical and mental health professionals are fond of pigeon-holing. To make a clinical diagnosis of an eating disorder, they want to fill in the boxes on their photocopied checklists. Body Mass Index under 18? Tick. No periods? Tick. Vomits three times a day? Tick. They want you to fit neatly into their diagnostic criteria so that they can give your eating disorder a specific name like anorexia.

The problem with this approach is that each person is an individual with an individual eating disorder. Some people have "textbook" eating disorders, but many, many more have combinations of behaviors and thought patterns that don't fit neatly under the common labels.

The first time I plucked up the courage to see my (not very friendly) doctor and confess that I thought I had a problem, she told me that I didn't have an eating disorder because I didn't fit her criteria. Never mind that I hated my body, was terrified of eating and was losing four pounds a week, because my weight was not yet below the threshold in her archaic diagnostic guidelines, I wasn't *really* in trouble. Of course, by this time I had decided I quite fancied being labeled "an anorexic" and so, frustrated by my doctor's attitude, I proceeded to go away and lose a couple more stone so that I could go back and get that last tick on her checklist.

Of course, this was many years ago now and I'd hope that doctors have better guidelines, better training and better bedside manners these days. But the fact remains that your worries about food, eating and your body should be taken seriously, even if you don't fit neatly into the anorexia, bulimia or binge eating disorder categories. You don't need to match anyone's criteria. If you're unhappy and worried about food, eating and your body's size, shape and weight, then you're in the realms of the eating disorder.

Knowing who gets eating disorders

Fat or thin, male or female, young or old, gay or straight, black or white, rich or poor, educated or unschooled: anyone, and I mean anyone, can suffer from an eating disorder.

You've probably heard that the most likely candidates to develop an eating disorder are white, middle-class teenagers whose parents are too demanding, controlling and/or abusive. Frankly, I'm not interested in generalizing statistics that attempt to put people in nice, neat compartments. I don't think it's particularly useful to tell a 40-something mother who's struggling with anorexia or a young gay guy who can't stop binging that they're not the norm. Don't they feel enough of a freak already?

Eating disorders are all around you, and they're on the rise. At the same time as it pushes the negative messages that reinforce low self-esteem and ridiculous ideals of beauty, the media delights in exposing celebrities suffering from eating disorders. No doubt you can reel off a list at breathtaking speed of famous Ed sufferers: Princess Di, Renee Zellweger, Victoria Beckham, Elton John, Nicole Richie and so on.

But the truth is, Ed isn't the preserve of the rich and famous. Ed can affect anyone, anywhere, anytime. However isolated you feel, there's bound to be someone nearby who's struggling too: a friend, a colleague, a neighbor, the guy behind you in the queue in a coffee house. Because so many people guard their Ed secret closely, it's really impossible to tell just who's suffering.

The important thing to remember is this: you're not alone.

Getting to know Ed's mates

Ed's a sociable sort and often invites various friends to join the party. Here are some other problems that may accompany an eating disorder:

- Alcohol and drug abuse: This can range from the occasional binge drinking episode and dependence on cannabis right through to alcoholism and addiction to hard-core drugs.
- Anxiety: A common problem for Ed sufferers. You may suffer from a dry mouth, the sweats or shakes, palpitations, a churning stomach and, at its worst, full-blown panic attacks.
- Attention-seeking behavior: It's no coincidence that many celebrities have eating disorders (and/or drug addictions, alcoholism, depression and so on). Celebrities need attention, to be seen. Some people with Eds have a similar need and they create drama so that they're the center of attention as much as possible.
- Compulsive lying: The line between reality and fantasy can blur as you weave a web of deceit to protect others from the truth of who you really are and how you really feel.
- Depression: You perpetually feel down, lifeless and detached from the world. You don't seem to care about anything or anyone, least of all yourself. The world is dark and hostile. It's a battle just to get out of bed in the morning.
- Obsessive-compulsive disorder (OCD): You absolutely have to carry out that ritual, put things in that order or check things again and again, otherwise some unthinkable horror will occur.
- Overspending: You spend money like you binge on food: recklessly, quickly and in great volumes.
- Promiscuity: In your need to be seen, held, loved, you let others use your body for their own gratification, caring little about how you feel.

- Self-harm: You hurt your body as a way to express your inner pain. You may kick, punch, scratch, bite, burn or cut yourself, usually on parts of the body you can hide from prying eyes under clothes.
- Self-imposed isolation: In your fear of people and public places, you become something of a hermit, hiding inside and avoiding contact with people as far as possible.
- Sleep disturbance: You may suffer from insomnia, constant sleepiness, nightmares and night terrors.
- Suicidal thoughts: The most dangerous of all Ed's mates. You think about walking in front of a bus or, in the worst case, you may actually try to take your own life, either as a cry for help or because you really can't see the point in living.
- Workaholism: You bury yourself in your work as a distraction, putting in ridiculously long hours and becoming obsessed with your job or studies.

If you have an eating disorder then one, two or perhaps many of these probably ring true for you. After all, Ed isn't an isolated problem with unique causes; it's an expression of your inner pain, confusion, anger and fear, as are all of these other problems.

Ultimately, letting go of Ed goes hand in hand with letting go of every other painful behavior, habit and illness you may have. Why? Because all these other problems stem from exactly the same place inside. Confront the root causes of your eating disorder and you'll also be confronting the reasons behind your depression, your insomnia, your self-harm and so on. And when you're ready to let Ed go, you can also find release from the other behaviors, illnesses and habits that are holding you back and making your life a misery.

So don't bother worrying about that big list of problems you have. The problems themselves don't mean anything at all; it's their cause that you need to look into.

2

Drawing on your strengths

So you've realized you have an eating disorder, and that you want rid of it. Now what? Well, before you can move forwards you need to get into the right frame of mind. And that means tapping into some essential inner resources that will see you through the ups and downs and twists and turns of your healing journey.

Having faith

The first step in letting go of Ed is believing that you can do it. Recovery is all about faith.

Faith is uplifting, strengthening, comforting, empowering, inspiring. Faith makes the darkest gloom brighten, the sharpest pain soften. Faith disperses your despair, your hopelessness, your negativity. Faith gently lifts your weary, bowed head and shows you the way forward, the way to a happier future. Faith makes the impossible possible.

Unfortunately, faith is also a bar of soap in a warm bath: a slippery bugger. No sooner have you got hold of some hope than it seems to slip right through your fingers, leaving you struggling to see a way out of your Ed-shaped prison.

First, be reassured that you aren't alone in your fight to find and keep faith; you're only human, after all. Sometimes you'll be in Eeyore mode, gripping a glass that's decidedly half-empty, and that's okay. Accept that, even though in these moments you've lost hope, in time you'll feel differently again.

And when faith is a fickle friend, hold fast to the fact that other people have healed from an eating disorder, and so can you. As impossible as the task may seem, as insurmountable as the obstacle looks, trust me when I say that letting go of Ed *is* within the realms of possibility.

Do you remember Kim Casali's comic strip *Love is...*? Well, here's my version for anyone recovering from Ed:

- Faith is... picking yourself up when you fall down, dusting yourself off and trying again.
- Faith is... focusing on your dreams and not worrying about the ups and downs you encounter on your path to the future you want.
- Faith is... believing that someday, somehow, you'll feel different inside and you won't need Ed anymore.
- Faith is... accepting that it may take you weeks, months, years to heal, but you'll get there.
- Faith is... saying, "I *can* do this and I *will* do this when I'm ready."

If you want to let go of Ed, you can. No matter how bad it gets, there's always hope.

Redirecting your courage

There's no doubt that letting go of your eating disorder is an absolutely terrifying prospect. The fear is utterly crippling. To walk away from Ed means to face some very scary, painful stuff, and it's no wonder that all too often you'd prefer to hide, trembling, under your bedcovers than roll your sleeves up and launch into battle with those scary demons.

You may doubt that you have the courage and the strength to beat Ed. These are the kind of thoughts that probably run through your mind:

- I've given into temptation and binged again. I'm so *weak*.
- I haven't been running today. I'm so *lazy*.
- I've had 200 calories more than I should. I'm *pathetic*.

- I lied so I wouldn't have to eat out with my friends. I'm a *coward*.

Actually, rather than proving that you're a weak, weedy person, Ed does the exact opposite. Having an eating disorder takes a huge amount of determination and courage. The truth is, you show an amazing amount of strength in controlling and overpowering your mind and body. Consider the following:

- You eat nothing all day, even though your stomach is hollow and hurts with hunger, your head is pounding and you feel faint.
- You say no to the huge slice of birthday cake a friend offers you, even though you want it so much.
- You binge and, even though it hurts your stomach and throat and makes you feel really tired, you force yourself to purge again and again.
- You do another ten minutes on the treadmill or another two lengths of the pool, even though your body is screaming that it's too much.

If you have an eating disorder, you'll know exactly what I mean when I say you have to fight very, *very* hard to maintain control. So you should also see that inside you already have plenty of courage, strength and drive. What you need to do now is take all that power you give to Ed and redirect it at recovery.

Accept that there will be good days and bad days; that sometimes you'll feel empowered and brave, and other times you'll be cowed by fear. Being afraid is perfectly normal and okay; it's how you handle the fear that matters. As Nelson Mandela said, "The brave man is not he who does not feel afraid, but he who conquers that fear."

Believe that you have the courage and accept that you will move through your fear when you're ready.

Trusting your intuition

Somewhere inside you is a very gentle but wise voice that always, always tells you the right choice to make. Even though that voice may be super quiet or dominated by stronger, more opinionated parts of you, trust me when I say it's there.

This is the kind of thing the voice inside may say:

- I don't like the look of that bloke over there who's looking at you; steer well clear.
- I don't think that job is right for you; you'll be bored within a week.
- You can trust your friend; she won't let you down.
- If you move house, you'll feel better inside.

Call it what you will—intuition, gut feeling, instinct—but this very powerful, nurturing part of you can really help you on your road to recovery. Learning to tune into that voice, listen and then have the courage to follow its wisdom isn't easy, but it's an essential part of getting well.

I find it very reassuring that this part of me knows what's best and that if I follow its guidance I'll always be okay. But it took me a long time to get to the point that I felt I could trust this part of me. Why? Because sometimes your intuition tells you things you just don't want to hear!

For example, say your intuition is telling you that a particular friendship or relationship is contributing to your Ed and you need to step back and get some breathing space. Deep down you know that the voice inside is speaking the truth, but following its guidance is just too scary. You love your partner/friend/family member, you don't want to hurt them and you're scared to be alone, so you cling on regardless. But how long can you carry on, knowing that you aren't doing what you really need and want inside? The answer is, not long. You may be able to bully the voice or ignore it for a while, but that patient part of you keeps on talking. And you know that the only way to feel better inside is to put your faith in your instincts.

Connecting to and following your intuition puts you on the path that's right for you: the path to peace, happiness and freedom from Ed. But don't be dispirited if you struggle to befriend that inner voice. In time, you'll build trust.

Keeping a sense of humor

You may have glanced at the heading to this section and recoiled in horror. Surely she's not mentioning the H word in a book about eating disorders? How inappropriate! Eating disorders are so awful, so destructive, so painful. What humor can she possibly see in them?

Well, it may be a rather controversial approach to Ed recovery, but I firmly believe that a sense of humor is key to healing. Seeing the funny side sometimes doesn't belittle the seriousness of your illness or the severity of your pain, but it sure makes Ed just a little more bearable.

A good friend of mine battled anorexia, bulimia and binge eating for many, many years. Emily wins all competitions for getting as close to death as possible before pulling back, time and time again. For so much of her life she was in a living hell. And yet throughout it all she kept her wicked sense of humor, until one dark, dreadful day when she lost all hope, all ability to see the lighter side. Her motto in life since that day has been this: "I lost my sense of humor once and they sectioned me." Every day, Emily remembers the distressing outcome of losing her ability to laugh and smile, and now she holds onto her sense of humor through thick and thin. And man is she a funny lady!

Sometimes, no matter how bad things are, you've just got to laugh at yourself, at your situation, at the world, at life. Ever so occasionally, can you catch yourself smiling rather than sobbing at your Ed?

I remember clearly the first day humor pierced through my

agony. I was feeling terrible—upset, panicky, desperate—and was preparing to numb it all with a binge on cheese, chocolate, pastries and bread. Yet as I looked at the array of food laid out on my bed in front of me, I had the pervading sense that something was missing. I had all my four favorite "naughty" foods, so what was holding me back?

Suddenly, I remembered a story my grandmother (Nanna) is fond of telling. I was a tiny wee tyke, in my highchair, and she was feeding me tea. I was being particularly belligerent and was demanding more food, more food. As she tells it, Nanna patiently held out her hand in front of me and counted off the foods I'd eaten on her fingers. "Now, Philippa," she said. "You've had a ham sandwich (counts one on her finger), you've had grapes (two), you've had some apple (three) and you've had a biscuit (four). How can you have room for more?" By this time Nanna was holding out four fingers. And after a short ponder, I piped up with, "But what about the thumb?"

Sitting on my bed, swirling in the panicked cyclone of pre-binge emotion, I suddenly found myself giggling. That little girl buried deep inside of me was being as cheeky as ever and demanding treats to fill fingers and thumbs: four types of food was still not enough. Did the release of laughter induce a miraculous, bolt-from-the-sky change in me and cause me to pack up the foods and choose not to binge? No, that day I still went ahead and binged: I needed to and I wasn't ready to stop. But somehow, in some small way, I felt just a little less sad, hated myself just a little less. And after a day filled with pain and exhausting behavior, it was that moment of humor I held onto as I lay in bed that night.

Of course, any kind of laughter is healing. When you sit down on a deckchair and it collapses, laugh. When Aunt Margery has one too many sherries and does a one-woman conga around your dining table, laugh. When your toddler nephew solemnly tells you he's off to the zoo to see the "flingymos," laugh, laugh, laugh.

You dedicate enough of yourself to serious, weighty, depressing issues. Once in a while, let it all go.

3

Laying the foundations for recovery

Your entire recovery rests on one essential quality: honesty. Run from the truth of your Ed and you'll never be able to let go. But find the courage to face up to your eating disorder and its causes and to focus on what you really want, feel and need inside and you're on the path to health. This chapter contains some of the first steps on the road to freeing yourself from Ed: the foundations on which you'll build your recovery.

Admitting the truth about your Ed

Before you can begin to recover from your eating disorder, you have to fully accept that you have it in the first place. Just like an alcoholic at their first AA meeting, you need to say to yourself, "My name's x and I have an eating disorder."

Then, once you can admit that you have an eating disorder, you need to accept just how bad it is. It's no good burying your head in the sand and pretending that you're okay when you aren't. Glossing over the severity of your problem doesn't help you tackle it. As difficult as it is, you need to take a long, hard look at Ed.

Ask yourself some probing questions:

- How long have you had an eating disorder?
- Can you remember a time when you didn't feel/behave this way, or have you always had issues with eating and your body?
- How has your eating disorder progressed? Has it got better, worse or stayed the same?
- How is your eating disorder impacting your day-to-day

life?

- How do you feel about having an eating disorder?
- How do you feel about recovering from your eating disorder?
- How do you see the future? Will you get better, worse or stay the same?

When you're ready to answer these questions honestly and fully, you can see where you stand with Ed and you'll know the exact nature of the beast you're battling. Facing up to the truth of your situation isn't easy, but it's the first step to a life without Ed.

Taking responsibility

When I was struggling with Ed, if anyone said to me, "You must take responsibility for yourself," I'd bristle like a threatened porcupine. *How dare you speak to me like that!?* was my usual (albeit silent) reaction, *I'm doing my bloody best here. Get lost!*

It was only years later, when I could look back on my illness from a place of healing, that I began to really understand what taking responsibility means and how important it is.

To put it bluntly, Ed is your problem and no one else's. You own Ed. You invited your eating disorder in, gave it a home and now wrestle with it day in, day out. Your relationship with Ed is intimate, personal, unique to you. And therefore you, and only you, can sever that relationship, can show Ed the door.

None of this detracts from the fact that other people may have hurt you badly, and it's that hurt that caused you to let Ed into your life and perhaps still causes you to hold fast to your behaviors. But as much as you want to, you can't blame anyone else for Ed. On some level you chose to have an eating disorder, and you won't be able to let go of Ed until you really own your problem and accept that you alone have the power to change things.

Before you hurl this book across the room in fury or despair, remember that I'm not suggesting that taking responsibility is at all easy. It's damn hard, it takes a lot of courage and you won't move forwards overnight.

It took me many, many years to sit comfortably with the R word. I was furious with the people who had hurt me so badly, who had caused me to feel such self-hatred, such grief, such desperation that I'd turned to Ed just to survive. I waited and waited for someone to rescue me from my pain and my illness: for a boyfriend to kiss it all away, for a therapist to wave a magic wand, but most of all for my father to somehow undo all those years of damage and make it all better inside me.

Unfortunately, that little word "fault" crept into my mind and festered there. It wasn't *my* fault I'd been screwed up so badly I'd ended up depressed, suicidal and desperate. It wasn't *my* fault I'd been wronged so badly that I'd resorted to Ed. It wasn't *my* fault I had an eating disorder, was it, so why should I take responsibility for it? The people who'd damaged me so badly, they're the ones who were responsible.

But in time I came to differentiate between who was responsible for causing the pain that gnawed at me and who was responsible for me, my life, my health, my wellbeing, my future. Blaming other people for Ed and expecting them to miraculously heal me wasn't getting me anywhere. I was no longer a small child, unable to protect myself from abuse; I was now a woman and I could choose the path before me. Ed was my creation, my special friend and my responsibility.

Don't be dispirited if it takes you a very long time to feel comfortable with this idea. But have faith that, when the time's right for you, you'll be able to grab hold of Ed and claim it as your own. And when you do, even though it may seem that you've connected yourself to Ed, you'll actually be taking a huge step away from it.

Concentrating on you

Somewhere inside there lives a person who knows how to let go of Ed: knows what's behind the terrible pain that makes you turn to your behaviors, and knows what you want and what you need in order to heal. Unfortunately, that person may well be buried, locked up, beaten into submission, ignored, ridiculed and distrusted by the Ed part of you.

When you're ready, you'll start to open your mind to that little voice inside, to believe that it's telling you the truth, to trust that it's guiding you towards freedom and peace. You'll begin to trust in yourself, in your instincts and in your right to do whatever it is that *you* want and *you* need.

All too often, we mistakenly think that meeting our own needs is selfish, that we must live our lives for other people, keeping them happy. What does it matter if we get hurt, as long as we don't rock the boat, as long as we don't make someone angry or sad or hurt?

Say you're going to a family party. You really, really don't want to go and a voice inside is screaming, "Please, get me out of this. I feel so ill and I know that this party will make me much worse. I'll put on an act and pretend I'm fine, but inside I'll be in agony. People will say and do hurtful things, and I'll just smile and be polite, friendly, easygoing. But then when it's over, when I'm back home alone, the pain will overwhelm me. I'll be worse, much worse in the days that follow."

But another voice comes back with, "Shut up! You have to go. If you don't your family will be cross and hurt. You'll cause all sorts of problems and they won't understand why you don't want to go. Pull yourself together, grit your teeth and get on with it. It's much easier that way. How can you even think of letting them down? Stop being so selfish."

Does this kind of battle strike a chord? Oh what misery this inner dialogue creates. You know what you need to do to stop people hurting you and to cushion yourself from Ed, but you just can't do it. It's too scary, too hard. You're terrified that by meeting your own needs you'll be opening yourself up to attack from others, from people you care about. You want to be a "nice person", because then people will like you and love you, and not hurt you or abandon you. You keep your mouth shut, you go with the flow, you decide that it's better that *you* feel pain than others around you.

Quite understandably, you've created a defense mechanism that you believe protects you from hurt. But in time you'll come to see that this approach to life actually creates more hurt than it deflects. Why should you carry all this pain inside? What's so terrible about looking after yourself, about meeting your own needs? Is it really the end of the world if you aren't perfect, if sometimes you do things that other people don't like? Is being nice all it's cracked up to be? You may be avoiding confrontation with others, but are you really protecting them from your pain? How long can you carry on living a lie? Can you imagine how liberated, how happy, how at peace you'd feel if you were true to yourself, if you let yourself follow your own heart?

Don't get me wrong, I'm not advocating you become cold, callous and uncaring of others' feelings, that you start trampling on people in a bid to get your own way all the time, that you become *selfish*. But a dictionary definition of selfish is "being concerned chiefly with your own personal profit or pleasure at the expense of consideration for others." By meeting your needs, you aren't only thinking of fleeting, self-gratifying pleasure, you're thinking about what you really need in order to be well and happy. And you're certainly not acting without considering others; you think hard about how other people feel and then you make a balanced decision to do what's best for you.

The only way to let go of Ed is to focus on you: on what *you* want, on what *you* need. It may take you a long time to get to a place where you feel you can be true to yourself, but be reassured that it really is okay to live your own life, to follow your own dreams, when you're ready. You only get one life, after all.

Focusing on the problem, not the symptom

There are plenty of books out there that promise to help you "manage", "improve" or even "cure" your damaging Ed behaviors, but this isn't one of them. I deliberately avoid such discussion throughout this book, because *recovering is not about focusing on your eating, but on why your eating is disordered in the first place.*

Behaviors are the symptoms not the cause of your Ed, and you can't solve a problem by simply addressing its side effects. Imagine you wake one morning to find an angry, red spot on your leg that's itching like mad. You wash the spot, disinfect it and cover it with antihistamine cream. By bedtime, the spot has stopped itching and reduced in size and color. The next morning you wake up to find another angry, red spot on your leg that's itching like mad. You wash the spot, disinfect it and cover it with antihistamine cream. By bedtime, the spot has stopped itching and reduced in size and color. The next morning... You get the picture. You could go on forever treating itchy spots (while your legs fast adopt a polka dot look) or you could try to work out what's causing these spots in the first place. A quick peek at your mattress reveals that a meany yellow spider is calling it home. You catch the spider, release it into the wilds of your garden and—hey presto!—no more bites. By dealing with the cause, you remove the problem.

Because Ed behaviors are so painful, miserable and debilitating, it's easy to fixate on fighting them: trying to curb binging, reduce vomiting or improve your diet, for example. These are all worthwhile and important efforts, but you need to recognize that, ultimately, you won't banish your eating disorder by beating its symptoms.

It's inevitable that you'll devote a lot of time and energy to battling Ed behaviors; after all, fighting Ed is part and parcel of having Ed. But remember that any tiny step you can take towards identifying and working on the root causes that lurk behind Ed is a massive stride in the right direction.

Accepting your eating disorder, for now

As difficult as it is to accept (and believe me, it took me many years), you will only let go of your Ed behaviors when you no longer need them. This is a very hard truth to stomach when you want to get well and are fighting so damn hard to get better.

I sat in front of my therapist day in, day out, sobbing and raging that I was still ill. I was trying so hard to get better, so why wasn't it working? Why couldn't I just stop, just let it all go? Why were my behaviors getting worse, not better? After so many years and so much heartache, why did I still have an eating disorder? Why? Why?

The answer was very simple: *I had an eating disorder because I needed to have an eating disorder.* No matter how severe my behaviors were, and how badly they were impacting on my life, I needed to have anorexia or bulimia. I needed Ed to protect me from the terrible pain and help me cope with the swirling, overwhelming feelings buried inside.

Hating myself for having Ed got me nowhere, and try as I might, I couldn't bully myself into getting better. Finally, I came to understand that I needed to accept Ed, just for now. I wasn't accepting Ed forever. I was merely accepting that at this point in my life I needed to have an eating disorder, but that one day, once I'd tackled the underlying causes of my problems, I wouldn't need Ed anymore and I would be free.

If you accept that you need your eating disorder right now, you create space inside. You can take the energy you put into wrestling with yourself over having Ed and channel it into healing the hurt that's behind your eating problems.

4

Probing what lies beneath

As the author Alice Walker put it, "The most important question in the world is, 'Why is the child crying?'" You can't let go of Ed until you really understand why you have it, why you are so unhappy inside. And the only way you'll discover the origins of your eating disorder is to do some probing. Working out what's driving Ed is a hard task that requires a great deal of honesty and commitment. So be gentle with yourself as you read through the following sections, which take you through the most common causes of Ed. You may be surprised what you discover.

Exploring familial origins

Evidence suggests that eating disorders can run in families. So does that mean that Ed is in the blood? Well, it all comes down to the age-old nature versus nurture debate (genes versus environment). Some researchers suggest that the prevalence of eating disorders within a family mean there's a genetic link, but others believe that the family environment shapes the recurring Ed behavior.

Sadly, my family is all too familiar with eating disorders. Over the years several relatives have suffered from various forms of Ed. This suggests that my family is *predisposed* to eating disorders. Now, that doesn't mean it's inevitable that a member of my family will have an eating disorder; it means that we're more likely to turn to Ed as a coping mechanism than something else, such as alcohol or drugs. Perhaps our genes direct us towards Ed; perhaps we all grew up in similar environments and so think in similar ways; perhaps eating disorders are too much the norm in my family and seen as the appropriate way to express pain. Whatever the reason, Ed seems to be an unwelcome and clingy family friend.

Take a close look at your family. Can you identify any eating disorders (of any level) in your family, past or present? You're not necessarily looking for extreme Eds here. Perhaps your mother is a lifelong diet addict or your obese aunt is a habitual comfort eater? Look at your male relatives as well. Do they have a healthy relationship with food and their bodies? Is Ed a common language in your family?

Thinking about your family's relationship with body image and eating may bring surprising discoveries that help you understand why you've chosen Ed to help you cope. And if you discover that your eating disorder relates to your family, you can then understand that letting go of Ed will mean choosing to reject your family's legacy. And who knows, in doing so perhaps you'll inspire other family members who are also struggling with Ed.

Delving into the past

Often, letting go of Ed requires exploration of painful issues from your past. Many people use eating disorders as a way to handle difficult emotions stemming from past events such as:

- Abandonment (physical or emotional)
- Abuse (sexual, physical and/or emotional)
- Family breakdowns
- Loss of a loved one
- Rejection
- Trauma (such as a violent attack)

The seeds of Ed are frequently sown in childhood. As I mention in other chapters of this book, Ed isn't just a way of behaving, it's a way of thinking. And Ed thinking can begin at an early age.

For example, I can trace my Ed thinking back a long, long way. My mother died when I was a tiny baby, leaving me with a struggling father who used abuse as a coping mechanism. As a young child I struggled with overwhelming feelings of fear, sadness, loneliness and anger. Unable to express my feelings in a safe, loving environment, I locked them away inside and developed a way of thinking and behaving that helped me manage my pain. At the age of eight, my Ed thinking involved a need to check things constantly, to drive my fingernails deep into my legs, to maintain silence around other people as far as possible and to discreetly discard my uneaten packed lunch in the school bin. By 18, Ed had evolved into obsessive-compulsive behaviors, episodes of starving and binging, and cutting my arms.

Recovering from Ed meant letting that small, abused, lonely child inside me have a voice at last. It meant really accepting the reality of my past and finally allowing myself to feel and then release the deeply painful feelings I was holding onto.

When you're trying to fathom the causes of your Ed, look backwards. Ask yourself whether the past is haunting you, whether painful feelings from things that happened years ago are as raw and real today as they were then. Try to trace back when your Ed thinking began. Is there an event you can associate with the onset of your pain? Only once you understand where the pain inside has come from can you start to unravel the feelings you're still carrying today and begin to let them, and Ed, go.

Examining control

Control is a big factor in eating disorders. An Ed sufferer usually feels that their life is dangerously out of control. This is truly terrifying, like being on a rollercoaster with no restraints. You feel panicked, frightened and desperate.

Here are some examples of situations that can make you feel out of control:

- Someone you care about dies, or nearly dies.

- Someone abuses you (sexually, physically and/or emotionally).
- Your partner leaves you.
- Your parents split up.
- You lose your job.
- You move house.
- You become ill or develop a disability.

The fear is overwhelming and you desperately need to regain some control. Because you can't control the situation that's affecting you, you find something else to control: your body. By enforcing tight rules over what your body eats and how it looks, you feel calmer and more in control. The horrible panicky feelings subside and you understand that by controlling your body in this way you can also control those awful emotions that you just can't cope with.

The sense of control Ed gives you is heavenly, while it lasts. But the control is only ever short-lived, and very quickly the panic returns, often worse than ever. Soon you have to go to greater and greater lengths to control your feelings, and you realize that you're fighting a losing battle.

Can you recognize the role that control plays in your eating disorder? Can you remember what it was that made you feel unable to cope, what you needed to control but couldn't? If you can work out where the fear of losing control stems from, you can begin to tackle that fear head on. Then, one bright day, you'll wake up and discover that you feel calmer inside and that the need to control your body and your feelings is diminishing.

Uncovering perfectionism

Perfectionists set very high standards and are hard on themselves when they fail to achieve their (often seriously tough) targets. Being perfect is seen as the key to happiness: the way to get love, attention and acceptance from others.

Perfectionism and Ed go hand in hand. Ed sufferers are often big achievers: sports stars, A-grade students, high-earners, award-winners. Only the best will do. They aren't satisfied being a size ten; they need to be a size zero. They won't go to the gym and do a couple of half-hearted minutes on a treadmill; they'll run until their shoes are steaming. They won't lose a couple of pounds on a diet; they'll lose 30.

The need to strive for perfection comes from childhood. Often, a perfectionist didn't feel unconditionally loved as a child; they felt that they needed to earn their parents' love and attention by being good at something. Rather than being loved simply for who they *were*, the child felt that they were loved for what they *did*. Self-worth became tied up with achievement.

When you have an Ed, perfectionism can be a key driving force. You need to be special, rather than just average or normal. You need to be a "good girl" or "good guy" so that people can't hurt and criticize you. You need to be the best you can possibly be, so that people will see you and love you. Being you isn't enough: you need to be perfect.

During my youth, I was the queen of perfectionism. I was the golden girl at school, a model student who always needed to be top of the class. I worked ridiculously hard to gain A after A, getting up at 4am to revise before exams and studying until I dropped each night. It wasn't enough for me to do well; I had to exceed expectations. My teachers told me how clever I was, how far I would go. If only they had realized how much pressure I was under, how truly destructive my behavior actually was and where I was heading with this need to be perfect. If only someone had taken me aside and said, "You know what, Pippa? It's fine to get a B now again and make room for a little fun in your life."

Look back over your life and over the course of your eating disorder. In the past, did you feel that you had to be good or perfect to make others happy and to earn their love and approval? Do you push yourself hard and continually set yourself very high standards? How do you feel when you stuff something up: guilty, upset, angry? Do you have to do everything well or do you allow yourself to do some things just adequately (or even poorly)?

Admitting to your perfectionism is a good first step. From there, the more work you do on self-acceptance, the more you'll find destructive perfectionism fades as you allow yourself to just be who you are: an imperfect but loveable human being.

Considering power

Ed can affect your relationships with the people around you in various ways. People around you may:

- Be more caring and concerned
- Give you more attention
- Try not to upset you
- Struggle to understand what you're going through
- Feel worried and scared by Ed

Ed's effect on the people in your life gives you some power in your relationships. For example, the following may ring true:

- You felt unloved, but now that you're ill people are showing that they care.
- You used to feel invisible and unimportant, but now people notice you.
- You don't have to deal with people being angry with you because they're tiptoeing around you.
- You live in a separate, secret world that others don't understand and they can't touch you there.
- Your illness is upsetting someone you care about and you want them to feel that way because they hurt you in the past.

As hard as it may be to admit, Ed is a useful tool for manipulating people. *Manipulation* is a word that has negative connotations, but remember that everyone manipulates others from time to time. By accepting that you sometimes use Ed to get more power in your relationships, you're not casting yourself as a cold-hearted, nasty, Disney-style villain. You're just being honest with yourself and understanding how Ed helps you as you relate to people.

To let go of Ed, you need to fully recognize what it gives you and find a way to fulfill your needs in other ways. So, for example, if you discover that Ed is a tool you use to get the people you care about to show their love, you can work on that. You find other ways to receive love from those close to you, and you work on loving yourself more, which means you don't need the constant reassurance of others' demonstrations of love.

For now, just try to accept that one of the reasons you have an eating disorder is because it makes it easier for you to manage your relationships. As you start to deal with your feelings and accept yourself, you'll find that you no longer need this aspect of Ed.

Rooting out the need to punish

Ed and self-hate are bosom buddies. If you have an eating disorder, you don't like yourself much at all. You probably think that you're weak, stupid, pathetic, unlovable and a whole host of other adjectives that sum up that you're a bad, bad person. And what does your mind tell you bad people deserve? Punishment.

Ed isn't just a way to control your feelings; it's a way to punish yourself for being bad or naughty. If your Ed behaviors were nice, fun and nurturing, you wouldn't get the same release from them. Right now, you *need* to hurt yourself because it's the only way you feel better about who you are.

When it first became apparent that I had anorexia, I remember a bewildered relative saying to me, "But I don't understand. Why this, of all things? You've always loved your food." And, of course, that was the entire point. A common misconception is that Ed sufferers dislike food, but this is often the furthest thing from the truth. The vast majority of people with eating disorders passionately adore food and that's exactly why they choose to punish themselves with it. By denying yourself enjoyment of something you like so much, by either refusing the food or eating so much you don't savor it, you hurt yourself badly.

So why do you need to punish yourself in the first place? The simple answer is: because at some point in the past, you learned to believe that there was something wrong with you, that you weren't good enough *as you are*. Your interpretation of an event or someone's actions or words conveyed that you were bad in some way and you took the message to heart. Now, the only way you can find any peace inside from the nasty, abusive voice that shouts, "You're rubbish; you're useless; you're a terrible person," is to punish, punish, punish.

The origins of this need to punish are often found in childhood. For example, for many years as a child I lived in a punitive environment in which I was constantly judged as a bad girl (usually) or good girl (very rarely). Because punishment formed a part of daily life, it became a normal way of life for me. So even when I left home and was free to live as I pleased, I continued to exist in cycles of judgment and punishment, because that, I felt, was what I deserved.

Look back over your past and try to identify the roots of your need to punish. They likely come from abuse, bullying or strict controls exerted on you. You can probably divide the past events that contribute to your self-punishment into two camps:

- You did nothing wrong at all. Someone attacked you for screwing up, but the truth is, you really didn't put a foot wrong. For example, you were three years old and you wet yourself while out shopping. Your father got very cross, told you what a disgusting child you were and made you stand in the corner when you got home. Were you a disgusting child? Did you deserve that punishment? No, no, no. You were a normal three year old who had an accident.

- You made a mistake. But instead of accepting that as the actions of a normal human being, the mistake was blown out of proportion. For example, you were six years old and playing boisterously with your brother when you knocked over your mum's favorite vase, smashing it. You were scared to tell your mother because you knew she'd be cross, so you hid the vase. Later, your mother discovered the broken shards and hit the roof. She yelled that you were bad, slapped you hard around the face and sent you to your room without dinner. Okay, so you needed to learn to own up to mishaps, but did the punishment fit the crime? No, you made a mistake, but you didn't deserve that level of punishment. Were you bad? No, your *behavior* may have been bad, but *you* certainly weren't. You were just a child behaving perfectly normally for your age.

Does any of this strike a chord? Can you remember times in the past when someone else's actions or words made you feel worthless or bad? Can you re-evaluate that situation now and consider whether you really deserved to feel that way? And do you still deserve to punish yourself now?

When you look back at the past, pay careful attention to punishments you may have had that related to food. These connect directly to your choice to use food as a punishment today. For instance, as a child I had to eat separately from the rest of the family, was often restricted to bread and water, and was once force-fed to the point of choking. It was only after years of suffering from Ed that I realized my eating behaviors were actually replaying the abuse of my childhood all these years later. A very painful truth to accept, but one that helped me realize I didn't want to hurt myself as I had been all those years ago.

Moving away from the need to punish happens when you begin to acknowledge the truth about your past, process the hurtful feelings and build a better relationship with yourself. At first, living without punishment feels strange, but boy is it a wonderful relief!

Looking at body changes

Ed involves controlling your body, so it stands to reason that an underlying cause for an eating disorder may be your feelings about your body.

From the moment we're conceived to the moment we die, our bodies are constantly changing. But that doesn't mean that we always happily accept this. Various changes can spark off out-of-control, unhappy feelings:

- Puberty: Many researchers believe that the drive to be underweight connects to a desire to revert to a pre-pubescent shape. In women, monthly bleeds, widening hips, swelling breasts and the natural weight increase that puberty brings can be frightening and unwelcome. Boys often shoot up and become lanky, even awkward looking. Emotionally, you may crave returning to childhood, when life seemed simpler, and you may want to force your body to be smaller and less sexual.
- Pregnancy: As much as you love the child growing inside you, you may find it hard to accept the changes that your body goes through during and after pregnancy. You may find yourself bent over the toilet regularly, and not by your own volition. Day by day, you seem to swell up, with larger breasts and nipples, curvier thighs and bottom, and a huge belly. Your appetite rockets and your eating tastes

transform. And after birth, your body doesn't snap quickly back to its pre-baby shape. You may find yourself gazing in the mirror at stretch marks and saggy skin.

- Middle-age spread: It's a fact that your metabolism slows as you age. In your 20s you may have been toned, slim and able to eat burgers and chips without a care in the world, but in your 30s and 40s you find you're softer, curvier and put on weight more easily.

- Menopause: The end of your fertility can be deeply distressing. Some women lose weight at this stage in life because they want control: rather than their body choosing to stop their periods, they want to stop the periods themselves by being underweight. Then, they feel, perhaps they can delay menopause. You also have to contend with myriad unpleasant symptoms and hormonal changes that can play a big part in how you feel about yourself and your body.

- Illness or injury: You may be lucky enough to go through your life without suffering any significant illness or injury until you fall asleep peacefully aged 99 and never wake up. But sadly, most of our lives don't follow this pattern. Dealing with illness or injury is a frightening and worrying experience, and it can unbalance your view of your body. For example, if you suffered from cancer, you may feel that you were invaded and couldn't control your body. And you may find it hard to accept the changes to your body that your illness brought, such as hair loss and scarring.

Eating disorders can be a way to deal with the difficult feelings that body changes bring up. Can you see a connection between how you feel about your body and your eating disorder? Can you isolate a particular change in your body that triggered Ed?

By acknowledging your feelings and working on accepting

and loving yourself and your body, you can move past feeling scared and unhappy in your own skin. As with other parts of your life, you can let go of needing to be in control and just *be*.

5

Dealing with feelings

Ed is a tool you use to avoid painful feelings, to numb yourself. And so it follows that letting go of Ed means an end to blocking emotions and a start to really *feeling*. The ideas in the following sections can be pretty hard to swallow, but on the flip side this stage in your recovery is definitely the most rewarding as well. By working on getting in touch with your feelings, you'll step away from merely existing or surviving and begin really living.

Understanding the importance of feeling

Feelings are a double-edged sword. On the one hand, feelings like love, joy, peace, excitement and passion make life a wonderful experience. But on the other hand, emotions like grief, fury, terror and loneliness are unarguably miserable and painful.

At one time or another, we all dream of banishing unpleasant feelings from our lives and living in a lovely, safe bubble of warm, happy emotions. But if that were possible, how would we even know how happy and free we were? Because if you don't experience the hard stuff in life, you don't recognize the good stuff:

- If you never feel lonely, you don't appreciate being surrounded by laughter, friendship and love.
- If you never feel scared, you don't appreciate safety.
- If you never feel angry, you don't appreciate feeling calm.
- If you never feel unhappiness, you don't appreciate happiness.

I could go on, but you get the idea.

Often, people categorize feelings into good and bad. They're happy to feel the "good" emotions like calmness and love, but they desperately want to avoid "bad" feelings like anger, fear and sadness. In an effort to run from those "bad" feelings, they use numbing mechanisms like Ed. But such avoidance strategies aren't selective when it comes to numbing feelings: when you use an eating disorder to minimize your painful feelings, you also detach yourself from your happier feelings. So Ed may help you to feel less angry, sad or lonely, but Ed will also make you feel less joyful, passionate, loving and loved. Ed makes you into a robot that goes through the motions of life rather than really engaging with it.

The truth is, there's no good and bad when it comes to feeling: all feelings are a normal and essential part of life. Those "bad" feelings are just as important as the "good" feelings. You may not enjoy having certain feelings, but in time you'll see that experiencing the lows makes the highs so much more wonderful and exhilarating.

When you're ready to let go of Ed, you'll allow both the good feelings and the bad feelings to come. You'll feel happier, freer, lighter than you ever dreamed possible, and when times become tough and you struggle with less pleasant emotions, you'll be comforted and strengthened by the knowledge that soon, very soon, you'll feel great once more.

Facing your fear

Getting in touch with your feelings is the most important step for recovery from your eating disorder. Unfortunately, it's also the most terrifying.

You welcomed Ed into your life for a very good reason: because you have feelings inside that you feel you just can't bear. Here are some of the feelings that you may be using Ed to numb:

- Anger

- Fear
- Frustration
- Grief
- Guilt
- Hate
- Loneliness
- Loss
- Shame

And who can blame you for wanting to avoid feeling these uncomfortable, painful feelings? No one. Because the fact is, these emotions are completely overwhelming to you. Rather than feeling just a little cross, you feel utterly furious. Rather than being a bit scared, you're paralyzed by sheer terror. And rather than being a bit sad, your heart is torn to pieces by agonizing grief. The intensity of your feelings is truly frightening and to protect yourself you've grabbed hold of Ed with both hands and clung on, using your eating disorder as a kind of tranquillizer.

Before you can face your fear of these feelings, you need to forgive yourself for being scared in the first place. You have nothing at all to be ashamed of: your fear is entirely justified and natural. And as much as other people around you may not understand and recognize the depth and intensity of your feelings, you know just how overwhelming and terrible these feelings are.

Imagine a two-year-old girl, shuddering and sobbing as a huge, vicious, growling dog approaches. Would you chastise her for being frightened? Of course not; you'd comfort her and tell her that it's okay to be scared. And you must do the same for yourself now, because facing your difficult feelings is just as terrifying as being a tiny, defenseless child faced with Rex the evil Rottweiler.

Once you've accepted that your fear is okay and under-standable, you may find yourself saying, "But I just can't do it. I can't handle these feelings." That's okay; don't push yourself. You *can* get past your fear and you *can* feel these emotions, but gently, over time and when you're ready. You don't have to take a deep breath, rip open your heart and let all these scary, intense emotions loose. Little by little, baby step by baby step, you'll open the door a tiny crack and let the feelings come out slowly, gently and in manageable amounts.

Locating your feelings in relation to Ed

Guess what? You aren't alone in using food and your body to help manage your feelings. Everyone does it, from time to time.

Take a look at these common figures of speech:

- *Bring up* a feeling.
- *Chew* it over.
- Eat your heart out.
- Feelings *consume* you.
- Feels so bad you can *taste* it.
- *Food* for thought
- It's too much to *stomach*.
- Hard to *swallow*
- *Spew* out your anger.
- Spill your guts.
- *Swallow* your feelings.
- The feeling *devours* you.
- This feeling is *eating* away at me.
- What's *eating* you?
- You make me *sick*.

See how often we relate emotions to eating?

Emotions are often felt in the digestive system. When you feel scared, your mouth dries up and you find it hard to swallow. When you're angry or anxious, your stomach becomes a tight knot. When you're revolted or ashamed, your tummy churns and you feel nausea rising. And when your emotions become too much, your digestive system may respond with conditions like ulcers and irritable bowel syndrome.

It's little wonder, then, that in order to quash difficult feelings, we use food. In anorexia, you starve the body of food, thus leaving the stomach empty of emotion. In binge eating disorder, you feel all the emotions swirling in your belly and bury them under layer upon layer of food. And in bulimia you mix food with those churning feelings in the tummy and then exorcize both feelings and food in a torrent of vomit (which nicely matches the unpleasant nature of the feelings themselves).

Close your eyes and let an unpleasant feeling rise up for a moment. Where in your body do you feel your emotion? Where has it come from? In what part of your body does it hide and what path does it take as it rises? Often, you'll find that the feeling comes from deep down in your guts and as it comes up it follows the course of your digestive system: stomach to throat to mouth.

Once you've identified where you hold your difficult feelings, see whether you can connect how your Ed behaviors relate to those feelings. Does Ed help you keep the feelings buried? Does Ed cleanse you of the feelings? Does Ed make you feel like the feelings don't exist at all?

Now, when you find yourself carrying out an Ed behavior, you can recognize exactly what you're doing and why. And you can ask yourself what's going on behind the behavior, what feeling are you using Ed to manage? Are you really angry or sad rather than hungry? Even if you're not ready to feel the emotion Ed's blocking, you're making great progress if you can recognize that it exists.

Getting in touch with your feelings

So how do you go about connecting to the feelings you've long avoided? Well, you have two choices: go straight to the source or take a roundabout route.

First, the direct approach. By now, you probably have a fairly good idea of some of the feelings that you're burying, and you can focus right on them. For example, during my recovery I knew that somewhere deep down inside I was terribly sad about losing my mum. When the time was right for me, I began gently exploring how I felt by thinking about Mum, looking at pictures and talking with my therapist about her. The grief began to surface, and I slowly expressed my feelings of loss, abandonment, anger and sadness.

But sometimes, going straight to the root of the feeling is just too hard, because the feeling is too intense. In that case, you can work on the feeling in a less direct manner. You can do plenty of helpful, healing work by allowing yourself to feel the difficult emotion, but about something less painful. So, when I was unable to cope with thinking about Mum and feeling the pain specific to her loss, I would let myself feel sad about other things. By watching a weepy movie or listening to some emotive music, the tears would come. Thoughts of Mum may have flitted into my mind as I cried, but I didn't push myself to focus on them. Instead, I connected to a little of the general sadness inside me. By releasing some of this sadness in tears, I built my confidence in dealing with difficult feelings. Then, when I was ready, the prospect of dealing with deeper sadness seemed just a little less daunting.

Whichever path you take to accessing your difficult feelings, remember that there's no rush and no pressure. Just do what feels right for you.

Letting it all out

You've got in touch with a painful, difficult feeling. Now what?

All of your instincts will probably be screaming, "Nasty feeling alert! Numb it, quick!" You'll want to do whatever it is that helps you squash down difficult feelings: binge, purge, run on the treadmill, get drunk and so on.

Instead, see if you can express your feeling in a healthier, less destructive way. Here are some ideas:

- Beat the hell out of a teddy (don't have one? Go buy one!).
- Dig the garden.
- Get in bed, pull the covers right over your head and sob.
- Go for a very long, brisk walk.
- Grab some paper and scribble hard on it with crayons.
- Make a huge mess: rip up some magazines or throw the contents of your closet onto the floor.
- Put music on loudly and dance, stamp or fling your body about.
- Roll up a newspaper and whack it repeatedly on a chair, your bed, wherever, until you're completely exhausted.
- Scream, shout and swear.
- Sing at the top of your voice.

These are only ideas; you'll no doubt be able to think of many more that best suit you. Just make sure that the activities you do to release feelings are very physical. Rather than keeping the pain inside by inflicting it on your body, you need to eternalize all that energy and express the feelings.

Releasing activities are best done when you're alone and in an environment in which you feel safe. But if you need to vent and you're in a place where you don't feel safe expressing your feelings (such as in an office or on a train), try the following:

- Shout loudly inside your head.
- Lock yourself in the toilet and cry, rock your body or scream silently.
- Get a notepad and write, write, write.
- Move your body. Go for a walk, do some stretches, clench your fists or tap your feet.

If these strategies don't work, *never* be afraid to simply stand up and exit the situation you're in, and take yourself to a place where you're safe and free to express your feelings. Don't worry about what people think of you. Just do what you need to do in order to let these terrible feelings come out of you in a way that doesn't cause you harm.

Venting your feelings often feels a lot like physical purging. All those vile, nasty feelings swirling around in your stomach come spurting out of you in a messy, powerful surge. This can be pretty scary at first, but when you get used to expressing the feelings it can feel liberating and actually rather good fun. I still use my favorite releasing activity when I'm really, really cross: I throw breakfast cereal all over the kitchen floor and then stamp on it until it's dust. Satisfyingly messy without creating any lasting damage, very cathartic and a little childish: perfect for expressing my anger.

Learning to use alternate ways to deal with your difficult feelings takes time, a lot of time. Some days, you'll simply need Ed and no substitute will do, and some days you'll have a good stab at doing a releasing activity but then give in to Ed. But then other days you'll find yourself sitting in a sea of pulverized cornflakes, grinning, because you've managed to express a difficult feeling without resorting to Ed. And boy, are those days worth the struggle!

Sitting with your feelings

The previous section discusses releasing your feelings. However, there's no rule that says you have to *do* anything at all with your feelings. Instead of expressing feelings, you can simply feel them and then wait for them to pass.

This approach is known as "sitting with your feelings" and it may take you a while to get your head around it. It was certainly a long time before I embraced the idea that it really was okay to have a feeling but not do something about it.

To sit with your feelings, you need to recognize and accept the fact that emotions are transient. In time, feelings diminish, and they pass. So although you may be deeply afraid by the strength of a feeling, if you can find the courage to sit with that feeling, in time the intensity will lessen. Your mind always protects you and will only let you feel as much as you can bear.

When you first start to allow yourself to feel emotions from deep inside, they're likely to be pretty strong feelings. Say the particular emotion you're connecting to is anger. You may feel livid, furious, enraged. You may be scared that the anger will overtake you and you'll act it out, perhaps by hurting someone or yourself. But how long will you actually be in the grip of this ferocious, tempestuous anger? If you sit with the anger, you'll find that in time, probably sooner than you expected, it calms.

Sitting with feelings is a technique I use regularly, and it really does help. For example, even today I sometimes find other people's anger frightening. As a small child, anger was something to fear, because it heralded abuse and pain. So when I encounter anger now, occasionally I'll feel like that little girl again and will start panicking that the anger means something bad is coming. But instead of moving to express my panic or run from it, I find a quiet place and just sit. I tell myself gently that it's just a feeling and it will pass. Taking deep breaths, I wait. And soon (a little sooner each time, in fact) the panic dissipates and I feel safe once more, and able to deal with the person's anger from a healthy, adult perspective.

The next time an uncomfortable emotion surfaces, try to sit with it:

- Notice the feeling: *I feel sad.*
- Accept the feeling: I accept that I feel sad.
- Remind yourself that you don't have to act on the feeling: *Even though I feel sad, I don't have to do anything.*
- Tell yourself that the feeling won't last forever: *In time, this*

sadness will pass.

The more you're able to sit with your feelings, the easier it becomes. Your faith in your ability to feel difficult emotions without falling apart grows and grows. But sitting with feelings isn't easy, especially at the start, so be gentle with yourself. Don't beat yourself up when you're unable to sit with a feeling, but do celebrate every moment you are able to connect. By sitting with the difficult feelings, you're opening your heart to the really happy ones too.

Recognizing your progress

The hardest thing about letting go of Ed is experiencing the pain that lies beneath. But when it comes to eating disorders, the adage "The only way out of pain is through it" rings true.

Dealing with your feelings is hard, painful and exhausting. You feel as though you're taking one step forwards, then five backwards. Indeed, your Ed behaviors may get worse, rather than better, when you get in touch with a hurtful feeling. Miserable and dispirited, you may find yourself losing faith and doubting that feeling this bad can ever lead to something good.

Don't give up! Any single moment in which you're able to identify, feel, express and/or sit with a difficult feeling is brilliant, wonderful progress. Yes it hurts, and yes it's horrible that you have to go through this, but stick with it. One day you'll look back from a happier, calmer place and you'll be so thankful and proud that you were brave enough to feel the pain.

6

Letting go of limiting ways

Ed comes with a free gift: a pair of specs that colors your view of the world. Like a train that's stuck chugging along the same old track to the same old destination, your thinking becomes locked into narrow, depressing patterns. This chapter helps you recognize those limiting ways of approaching life and offers some happier, healthier alternatives. By breaking free from restrictive attitudes, you open your life up to freedom and peace, and take the wind right out of Ed's sails.

Coloring in black and white thinking

Ed separates the world into diametric opposites: fat and thin, good and bad, right and wrong, failure and success, safe and dangerous. This way of looking at the world is called black and white (all or nothing) thinking.

Black and white thinking is a very limiting, miserable mindset. Here are some examples of how it works:

- You decide that today is a good day if you eat nothing all morning. But at 10am, someone offers you a cookie, and you give into temptation. Now that you've been bad, you decide you may as well go the whole hog and be as bad as can be. You start to binge.
- You want to lose five pounds before a big party so that you'll look great in your new little black dress. You go on a soup-only diet and spend two hours in the gym every evening for a week. On the morning of the party, you try on the dress and it fits perfectly. Then you get on the scales and discover you've lost four pounds, not the five you

wanted. Disaster! You decide you've completely failed and you're too fat and ugly to go to the party. You stay home alone instead, and start planning your next diet.

- Your parents were very controlling when you were a child and put a lot of pressure on you to be the best at everything. Now you feel that they were complete failures as parents, that they got everything wrong all the time, that they never loved you, that they were bad, bad people. You can't see any good in your parents at all, and you blame them entirely for your eating disorder.

As you can see from these examples, black and white thinking robs you of the ability to see things in perspective. One cookie doesn't make you bad; you looked great in the dress and four pounds was an impressive weight loss; your parents made mistakes but they did some things right as well.

Much as you may wish it, you can't divide life neatly down the middle and categorize everything into extremes of negative or positive. Life is chaotic and complicated and ever-changing. Slowly, slowly, start opening your mind to the possibility that there's much more to life than black and white. When you do, you'll find struggling gives way to acceptance.

Dismissing shoulds and musts

When it comes to making decisions for yourself, strip the words *should, must, ought* and *have to* from your vocabulary. These words kill choices dead: they force you to pick just one of the options available.

Here are some examples of these restrictive words in action, and how a little rephrasing can take the pressure off:

- I should/must/ought to/have to visit my parents soon becomes If I want to, I can visit my parents soon.
- I should/must/ought to/have to run a mile on this treadmill

becomes I'd like to run a mile on this treadmill, but I don't have to.

- I should/must/ought to/have to say no to pudding becomes I can choose between saying yes or no to pudding.

When you stop thinking in terms of shoulds, you empower yourself and open up a whole world of liberating choices. Your life is your own and you really do have the right to choose the path that's best for you.

And letting go of that dictatorial mindset means you begin to take responsibility for your actions. Rather than placing the power with others, you're in charge of your life, which means an end to feeling trapped.

The first time I broke away from the shoulds and musts in my mind was one Christmas when I was battling anorexia. I felt I really *should* leave my student accommodation and go home for the holidays, because it was tradition and my family expected me to, but I knew that a week of false jollity and feasting would be hell on earth and would push me even further into my world of starvation and punishment. Finally, after weeks of worrying and dreading what was to come, it occurred to me that I had a choice: as much as it may upset them, I could just stay at home and decline my family's invite. What a terrifying but strangely liberating thought! So I scraped together my courage, picked up the phone and told my father I'd be giving Christmas a miss this year. Oh the relief. Of course, I faced a pretty tough few days on my own, but I accepted that. It was my choice and therefore, lonely or not, I was free.

Next time you catch yourself thinking a should or must, pause for a moment. Recognize that you have a choice in every situation. Of course on the surface there are countless shoulds: you should drive within the speed limit; you should brush your teeth; you should read a book from front to back. But on closer consideration you'll find they're all your own choices. You choose to drive within the speed limit to avoid causing an accident; you choose to brush your teeth to avoid tooth decay; you choose to read a book from front to back because it makes more sense that way.

Believing in your right to choose and finding the courage to break away from the status quo isn't easy. But when you're able to find the strength to make and own your choices, that's another nail in Ed's coffin.

Drifting away from drama

Some Ed sufferers are natural thespians: larger-than-life characters whose lives seem to be a series of dramas. They don't just misplace their front door keys, they get locked out in the height of winter in their pajamas. They don't just bake a cake, they set fire to the kitchen. And they're not late simply because they got stuck in traffic: their steering wheel fell off, they got shunted by a pedal bike, they were set upon by wild bears, and so on.

There's nothing wrong with a little drama; it makes for a much more interesting, entertaining life. Where a dramatic nature can lead you astray, however, is when it feeds your Ed.

Drama gets you and your eating disorder attention, and for this reason it can be highly addictive. Rather than quietly getting on with Ed and hoping no one sees how ill you are, you may find yourself doing the exact opposite: creating (either consciously or subconsciously) drama around your eating disorder to get people to sit up and take notice of your pain. For example, you may constantly be the center of medical emergencies or you may keep having very public, very spectacular meltdowns.

As you recover you can let go of Ed's need for drama. You are so much more than your eating disorder, and you'd prefer people paid attention to *you* rather than your illness. Ed is booed off stage and *you* take the spotlight instead. And you find that you need less drama, less attention. You're happier to enjoy a simpler life; rather than boring, mundane becomes quite enjoyable. Life becomes calmer, quieter, more peaceful. You're okay, just as you are.

Being unique rather than special

You may think that Ed is a passport to belonging, conforming, following the crowd. After all, everyone wants the "perfect body", right? Actually, Ed is the complete opposite: it's the struggle to stand out as different from the rest, unusual, special.

Why? Well, far from being the norm, the "perfect body" (as defined by society) is incredibly rare. Don't believe me? Go to a busy public place like a park, take a seat and watch the world go by. Look carefully at all the different bodies, their shapes and sizes. How many of the people passing by have a perfect body? Very few, if any.

Only a tiny proportion of the population conforms to society's ideals of what's beautiful. So when you're striving to become one of that minute minority, it's because you want to be more than average or "normal": you want to be special. And by *special*, what you really mean is *better*.

Ed makes you compare yourself to other people:

- Look, that guy's overweight. *I'm* not. I'm better than him.
- That woman's drinking orange juice. Doesn't she know how many calories it has? *I* only drink water. I'm better than her.
- My friend Jo is a size eight. Well, *I'm* going to be a size six then, so that I'm better than her.

Letting go of Ed means letting go of needing to be special, to be bigger, better, brighter than others, and being unique instead. Unique sets you apart but keeps you on the same level as other people, because we're all unique. Unique is quirky, original and individual. Unique says whoever you are and however you look, you belong in this world.

Let go of being special, of wanting to be better than others, of wishing you could join that elite of "beautiful people" who must lead such perfect lives (they don't). Just be you instead. It's a lot easier, and a lot more fun.

Finishing with fairy tales

Women are particularly drawn to romantic fantasies. That's why the romance genre is big business for publishers and movie-makers.

Ask yourself, have you ever read a book or watched a movie and wished you could leap into that imaginary world and become the hero or heroine? Maybe if you looked like the protagonist—slim, elegant, beautiful—then you'd have her happy ending too: money, success, a baby, walking into the sunset hand in hand with some gorgeous, adoring bloke.

Of course, there's nothing wrong with a little harmless fantasy. But when you start to believe a level of reality exists in this fairy-tale world, that's when you can come a cropper.

Being skinnier, or more toned, won't transport you into a fairy tale. Prince Charming won't ride up on his trusty steed to sweep you off your feet. Mr. Darcy won't come knocking at your door (and neither will Colin Firth, for that matter). And no handsome vampire will vow undying, eternal love for you and transform your life into one of melodrama and high passion.

By all means lose yourself in romantic, wonderful fantasies. It's a great way to unwind, and to find comfort and a sense of love. But keep your feet firmly on the ground as you dream. The stories in your head, on paper or on screen are just that: stories, not realities. And attempting to transform your body so that you resemble a fictional character will not lead to a happy-ever-after ending.

Rejecting victimhood

In every relationship we play roles, and a favorite role that Ed sufferers adopt is the victim.

When you're a victim, you let go of all responsibility. You see yourself as innocent, vulnerable, wronged, *victimized* by someone you cast in the role of perpetrator or aggressor.

Victimhood can feel safe when you have an Ed, but it doesn't serve you at all. By being a victim, you give all your power away. The victim is defenseless and vulnerable, and the aggressor is firmly in charge.

A dictionary definition of *victim* is "someone who's come to feel helpless and passive in the face of misfortune." Do you want to be helpless and passive? In the past, you may have suffered terribly at the hands of others. But that doesn't mean you have to keep giving those people the power to hurt you by being a victim.

Instead of being a victim, try to see yourself as a survivor: strong, proud and powerful.

Releasing control

Try as you might, you can't control life. And when you have an Ed, that's pretty scary. But what if you could go from fearing life's roller coaster path to accepting and even enjoying it?

You want certainty in your life, to feel settled and calm and safe. But the only certainty in life is change. Therefore, the only way to feel settled and calm and safe is to accept the ever-changing nature of life.

The key to letting go of your desire to control life is adopting a que será será attitude. No matter what happens, *you are exactly where you're meant to be right now in your life*. You may not like how your life looks today, and you may wish it looked different, but you can trust that you're in the right place at the right time.

Step back and go with the flow, trusting that life will take you where you're meant to go. Imagine life as a giant ocean: lie back and float, riding the natural rhythms of the waves, up and down, up and down. Stop fighting life and just let it happen. Everything will be okay.

7

Finding yourself

Now for the really fun bit. It's time to stop being safe. It's time to stop hiding you, the real you, behind Ed. It's time to get to know who you are: your likes, your dislikes, your strengths, your weaknesses, your passions, your fears. And it's time to start accepting, liking, even loving you.

Sound scary? Consider this point made by writer Marianne Williamson:

> Our deepest fear is not that we are inadequate. Our deepest fear is that we are powerful beyond measure. It is our Light, not our Darkness, that most frightens us. We ask ourselves, who am I to be brilliant, gorgeous, talented, fabulous? Actually, who are you NOT to be?

Keep in mind these reassuring truths. First, the world doesn't end when you reveal who you really are; actually, life gets a lot better, not worse. Second, being yourself is simply the best feeling in the world: the key to inner peace, balance and happiness. And finally, in finding yourself, you lose Ed.

Taking off your Ed mask

If I ask you who you are, what's your automatic response? An anorexic? A bulimic? A binge eater? Someone who's struggling with an eating disorder?

In this book I steer clear of the terms *anorexic, bulimic* and *binge eater* because they're labels. You aren't an anorexic; you're someone who has anorexia at this time. You aren't your eating disorder; you're so much more. Ed is just a tiny part of the amazing, complex person you are.

At some point in the past, you became frightened to be yourself: to show how you really feel, what you really want, who you really are. So you buried large parts of you, the real you, deep inside and you put on Ed's mask.

Now, a battle rages inside. You'd like to let go of Ed and release the parts of you trapped inside, because you know then you'll be happier. But you're scared to let go of Ed's protection. Taking off your Ed mask leaves you vulnerable. What if the real you isn't good enough? What if people don't like who you are? What if they won't accept you? What if you get hurt?

Being scared to show the world who you are is perfectly natural and okay. But in time you can move past your fears and see that you're completely acceptable and loveable *just as you are*.

No one expects you to just rip off Ed's mask one day with a grand flourish and declare, "Here I am, world, like it or lump it." As with all elements of your recovery, take it slowly. First, get to know you are and then, a little bit at a time, gently test out being yourself.

Discovering who you are

Who are you? There's so much to explore about yourself, and every detail you find out is empowering and liberating.

Get a huge sheet of paper (the biggest you can find) and write *Me* in the middle. Then all over the paper note down your characteristics, your likes and dislikes, your strengths and weaknesses, anything and everything that makes you, you.

Here are some examples of what you may write:

- Bit bossy
- Bubble bath addict
- Caring
- Don't like feeling tired
- Good listener

- Green-fingered
- Happy when I dance
- Hate parsnips
- Have no sense of direction
- Like walking on the beach
- Loud laugh
- Make a mean chili
- Not a fan of shoot 'em up films
- Rubbish at tennis
- Take criticism to heart
- Think slugs are vile
- Want to visit Rome

See how random and eclectic the list is? There are so many different aspects to you, each as great and acceptable and loveable as the next.

Keep adding to your *Me* sheet. Eventually, you'll start running out of room and then you can stand back and review your brainstorming. Look how much you've discovered about yourself, how much there is to you! Look how human you are: a blend of strengths and weaknesses, likes and dislikes.

Now take each of your notes in turn and ask yourself whether you can accept, or even like, that characteristic. Can you accept someone who's bossy from time to time? Can you like a person who's sensitive to criticism? Can you love your laugh, your slug aversion, your inability to hit a tennis ball? Can you be more than Ed? Can you also be someone who dances and walks on the beach and avoids parsnips at all costs?

If you're finding this difficult (and you probably are, so don't worry) try imagining that this person you've found out about is someone else, like a character in a book or a movie. People struggling with Ed are too tough on themselves. I bet what you're finding hard to accept about yourself right now you can accept, even like, in another person. Try it and see.

Loving all the different parts of you

There are many elements that make up your personality. For example, inside you have:

- A Child
- A Clown
- A Critic
- A Judge
- A Nurturer
- A Warrior
- A Worrier

... and much, much more.

When you have an eating disorder, these different parts of you struggle to live together harmoniously, and often some bits become more dominant than others. For example, your Critic may have grown into a damaging, powerful force that bullies other parts of you such as your Child and your Nurturer.

To end the war inside, you need to find a better balance. That balance comes when you start to listen to, value and accept *all* the different parts of you, even those bits that drive you nuts.

Imagine your mind is a room full of children, all clamoring to tell you their opinion. Soon you're in the midst of a headache-inducing cacophony of squabbles and shouting, and the only voice you can make out is that of the loudest child, who's completely ruling the roost. "Time out!" you yell. The children fall silent. Now you go around the group one by one, listening to each voice in turn, trying to understand where the child's coming from and thanking them for sharing their view. Peace prevails and the children settle down, happier and quieter because they feel heard and valued.

Treat all the different parts of you with compassion and respect. They're all valid, valuable parts that live in each of us. And if you're struggling to accept an especially dominating part, remember that a bully is really just an insecure person who needs to be seen, heard and loved.

Nurturing your inner child

There's one part of you that needs the most attention and love on your road to recovery: your inner child. Somewhere inside is a little child who's feeling hurt and frightened and angry and lonely and lost. And just like any child, they need your love, reassurance and support.

The best way to connect with your inner child is to visualize them. How old are they? What do they look like? What's their name? Then, once you've got a clear picture of your inner child, you can move onto exploring that little person's feelings and needs.

My inner child is the three-year-old me: cute, cheeky, loveable Pip. During my recovery, when I was trying to get to know Pip, I'd chat to her in my diary. A delve into an old journal turned up this, one of our early conversations:

Hello. How are you?
Sad and mad.
Why's that?
You hurt me. You ignore me. I feel lonely.
I'm sorry. I don't want you to feel lonely. I get caught up
    sometimes and forget to listen to you.
That makes me sad. I don't like being sad.
I don't want you to be sad. What would cheer you up?
Bubble bath. Sunshine. Smiles. Quiet. Fun. Pink wafer biscuits.
Okay. I can manage that. Friends?
Friends.

Conversations like this help you identify what your inner child is feeling and what they need from you. Then you can move onto acting in a way that helps, rather than hurts, that little child inside.

Here are some ways I respond to my inner child:

- When she's scared, I take her somewhere she feels safe, such as under the covers in bed.
- When she's sad, I lie down on my bed and picture myself spooning around her, holding her as a mother would a child.
- When she's angry, I let her release it in childish ways: I lie on the floor and have a good old, thrashing-about tantrum, scribble with a black crayon, throw some stuff about.
- When she's tired and overwrought, I cuddle under a blanket and have a nap.
- When she needs some fun, I play with her: stamp in rain puddles, read a children's book, draw a picture, blow bubbles.
- It doesn't matter what you do, as long as you're building a relationship with the child part of you.

By now, you may be thinking, "Talking to yourself? Imagining you're a child again? Behaving like a big kid? That's bonkers!" Yes, relating to your inner child can seem a bit nutty at first. But if you let go of your inhibitions and give this a try, you'll find the work you do amazingly enlightening, healing and even fun.

Accepting yourself now and as you grow

Throughout this book, I talk about self-acceptance as the key to recovery. You need to accept yourself, warts and all, in order to find peace inside. However, this acceptance doesn't mean that you have to give up on trying to grow as a person.

For example, say you're very scared of people's anger and so do all you can to avoid confrontation. You can accept yourself now, exactly as you are. It's okay that you get scared; you can accept that the fear is part of you. But that doesn't mean you intend to always feel this way: one day you want to let go of that fear and be someone who can handle conflict in a healthy way.

First you need to accept who you are right now, in this moment. Then you need to decide which aspects of yourself you'd like to work on, and which aspects you're happy to accept for good. So you may decide that you'd like to be less judgmental, but you don't mind being someone who's very driven.

To change or not to change, that is the question. Only you can decide what you'll accept about yourself and in which areas you want to grow. Let your intuition be your guide and keep in mind Saint Francis of Assisi's prayer:

Lord, grant me the serenity to accept the things I cannot change, the courage to change the things I can, and the wisdom to know the difference.

8

Looking forwards

Part of discovering who you are is getting in touch with your dreams. What do you want from your life? Where do you want to be in five, ten, fifty years' time? When you lie in bed at night and let your mind drift, where do your fantasies take you? Looking to the future can help focus your recovery in the here and now. And nothing cheers a gloomy day better than a daydream of a brighter place...

Embracing the future
The future can look pretty gloomy when you have an eating disorder. You picture yourself years from now, still battling. You wonder whether your health will deteriorate further; whether friends and loved ones will give up on you. Your dreams are a million miles away: if you can't even let go of Ed, how will you ever write that book, climb that mountain, meet that special someone, become a parent or look in the mirror without cringing? You lose hope that the future can be anything different than the painful past and the unhappy present.

But if you can find the faith inside to believe in a brighter, better future, you give yourself something to aim for. Making your goal simply *recovery* means very little unless you define what recovery will mean for you. What will your life be like when you let go of Ed?

I'm not suggesting that you make elaborate, concrete plans for the future. You can't control the future because you can't control life, and you'll invariably feel crushed when your nice, organized plans don't work out. Instead, I'm asking you to daydream, to let your mind slip away and conjure up lovely pictures of a future you'd like to live.

And when you can let yourself dream of that better future, you can use your dreams to help you discover who you are and where you want to go, and to guide and strengthen you in your recovery.

Visualizing a life without Ed

Lose yourself in dreams of a happy, healthy future. Fantasize about what life will feel like when you let go of Ed.

When I was healing, I wrote a *When I let go of Ed...* list. I wrote down my dreams and fantasies about life after Ed. Here are some of the things I included:

- I'll know that I'll always be okay and can get through anything.
- I'll take good care of the little girl inside me.
- I'll know I'm okay, just as I am.
- I'll forgive myself for making mistakes because they make me human and help me grow.
- Life will be fun!
- I'll write and write and write.
- I'll know I never deserve to be hurt or punished.
- I'll know which voice inside to follow.
- I'll dance and sing and laugh and walk in the park often.
- I won't be a good girl or a bad girl; I'll just be me.
- I won't have to be perfect anymore.
- I'll go for my dreams.
- It'll be quieter inside me.
- It'll be okay to cry.
- I'll know I'm a good person who deserves to be happy and loved.
- I'll stop looking outside myself for the answers.
- I'll accept my limitations.
- I'll trust my intuition.

- I'll slow down.
- Life will be simpler.
- I'll feel safe at last.
- I won't run from pain, but will sit with it and trust that I'll heal in time.
- Something wonderful will creep into the hole inside me and made me whole.

So has every one of these dreams come true for me, now that I've let go of Ed? The answer is, yes and no. Sometimes, I fulfill these dreams: I engage with life; I accept myself as I am; I feel at peace and content. And sometimes, I struggle a bit, because I'm only human, after all. But even when I lose sight of my "happy place", that's okay, because I know that it's there somewhere and I'll find it again soon.

Close your eyes and try to picture how your life will feel without Ed. What will your *When I let go of Ed...* list include?

Making a wish list

Having thought about how you'll feel without Ed, you can now begin to consider what you'll do with your life. When you let go of Ed you'll have so much more room in your life. Ed holds you back in the past, but when you recover you'll be free to explore that long, exciting future in front of you.

So what do you want from your future? Make yourself a wish list. Include anything and everything, from ideas for what you'll do tomorrow to what you'll do aged 90.

Here are some questions to get you started:

- Do you want to be in a relationship? Do you want to get married or live with someone one day?
- Do you want kids? What kind of stuff will you do with your kids?
- Where you do want to live?

- What will your home look like?
- What job(s) do you fancy doing?
- Will you have pets?
- Do you want to travel? Where to?
- What will family Christmases be like?
- What kind of clothes will you wear?
- What's the best birthday gift you'll ever receive?
- What secret ambitions do you have? Do you want to pursue them?

Remember, this is a wish list: an airy-fairy list of vague dreams and things that sound quite nice. It's not set in stone, and you can change it as often as you like; every hour, if you want. This exercise isn't about fixing firm goals for the future that you must achieve (for example, to be happy I must get married, have kids, live in suburbia and own a dog called Nigel); it simply helps you connect to the very idea of having a future. It opens up the possibilities and gets you feeling positive, excited and happy about all the wonderful things that may lie ahead for you.

Living the future right now

The point of dreaming about your future is to help you do the things now, today, that can help you live your bigger dreams. The point isn't to plan some utopian future and then live your life waiting for that future to manifest. As John Lennon said, "Life is what happens to you while you're busy making other plans." Don't waste your life waiting to live, live now!

Your life today may not look exactly as you want, but that doesn't mean you can't enjoy yourself and fully connect to the world. For example, as I write this I'm living in a house I don't particularly like. For months, we've had our house on the market, but have had a run of bad luck in selling it. It's very annoying and I long to feel settled in a nice new home. So you're probably thinking I must be pretty miserable now, what with all this stress and frustration? Not at all. I have moments when I get grumpy, but then I look at the bigger picture and appreciate all the other good things in my life. I'm not going to put off feeling happy until we've finally moved; I'm going to fling my arms wide and embrace life right now.

Each moment of life is really precious. The older I get, the more I appreciate just how young my mum was when she died (31), and how tragic it is that she didn't have longer. Remembering her makes me want to make the best of each day. Of course, often I don't. I waste an evening watching trash on TV and having a silly row with my husband over the remote control. But that's okay: I'm just being human. There are times when I can appreciate and enjoy the here and now, and that's good enough.

How many times have you looked back at a time in your life and thought, "Those were good days; why couldn't I see it then?" If you struggle to root yourself in the present and live life to the full right now, try getting some perspective. Play the deathbed game: picture yourself a snowy-haired old person who's about to slip peacefully away and is looking back over life. What do you want that future, older you to see: a colorful life, full of passion and laughter and tears and vivid experiences? Will you smile fondly as you recall all your memories, both happy and sad? Will you go to sleep happy in the knowledge that whatever life brought you, you really lived?

As Abraham Lincoln put it: "In the end, it's not the years in your life that count. It's the life in your years."

Considering your legacy to your children

As well as thinking about your own future to help inspire and direct you in your recovery, also think about your children's future.

You may already have children, or you may think that someday you'd like to have them. Either way, your children, here today or a yet twinkle in your eye, are a big part of your recovery.

Children learn by imitation, and their parents are their most influential role models. If your daughter grows up seeing Mummy constantly dieting and hating her body, it's a logical progression that your daughter will think that's normal and what's expected of her, and will grow up to also diet and hate her body. If your son grows up seeing Daddy yo-yoing between binge eating and obsessive gym workouts, he'll likely follow in Daddy's footsteps.

On the other hand, children can rebel and do their utmost to reject their parents' choices. But sadly, this rarely means a child who's grown up in a home where parents have disordered eating will grow up to have a happy, healthy relationship with their body and with food. Instead, the child of an anorexic may grow up to binge eat to the point of obesity. And the bulimic's child may grow up to self-starve.

Wanting what's best for your child, whether that child exists yet or not, can be a very powerful motivation for eating disorder recovery. No one wants their child to grow up to befriend Ed. We know only too well what a terrible life that is.

For me, wanting children fuelled part of my desire to let go of Ed. Having lost my own mother right after she gave birth to me, I was determined to be healthy and strong for pregnancy, birth and motherhood; to do my utmost to be there for my child. And I didn't want to be battling demons while a baby grew in my tummy, while I spoon-fed my baby veggie mush or when my toddler decided to share with me his half-chewed sandwich (yum!). It would take away so much of the magic and wonder of mothering I'd been looking forward to for my whole life.

But most of all, I wanted my child to grow up happy in his own skin. I wanted him to be confident and secure, and to love and accepted himself, as I would love and accept him. I wanted him to see food as nourishment, but no big deal, and his body as this great thing that lets him run and jump and splash and cuddle. I wanted him to grow up blissfully ignorant of self-doubt, self-hate and self-punishment, because no child deserves such demons to battle.

If you want children, or you have them already, ask yourself what legacy you want to leave for them. Could protecting your children be an added reason to work on letting go of Ed? Could it strengthen your resolve, and give you a focus to work towards?

9

Connecting with your body

Ed tells you that your body is something to be hated, feared, rejected, punished. For too long now, you've looked in the mirror and seen a fat, ugly, unacceptable body. But what's actually looking back at you is a perfectly normal, loveable body that's crying out for an end to the exhausting, painful abuse you subject it to. This chapter helps you see that letting go of Ed means rebuilding your damaged relationship with your body— slowly, gently, tenderly—and feeling safe and at peace in your own skin at last.

Stepping back inside your body

As a child, you lived inside your body. You accepted it, and were quite comfortable with the size of your nose, your ears, your stomach. Through your body you experienced a wealth of sensations: running down a hill with the wind in your face, swinging higher and higher to touch the clouds, licking an ice cream on a sandy beach. You had a great, healthy, happy relationship with your body. You gave it what it needed—food, drink, sleep and care—and in return it allowed you to do a million wonderful things.

But at some point your relationship with your body changed. You began to feel unhappy inside, and to project that unhappiness onto your body image. You started to look in the mirror and judge what you saw. Words like *ugly* and *fat* crept into descriptions of yourself. You began to think that if you could just change this or that about your body, you'd be happier again.

By now you'd stepped outside of your skin. Your body was an object, something you looked at from outside, something you needed to transform and control. You disconnected from your body, and that distance between you and your body made it easier to hurt yourself with Ed. When hunger gnawed at your insides, when your stomach ached, when your head spun, you could ignore the sensations. You felt your body, but in a distant, detached way.

For me, this disassociation began at an early age. Because I was being physically hurt by my father, I needed to find a way to cope with the bodily pain. Without knowing or understanding what I was doing, I began detaching from my body. I zoned out of the pain and let myself drift up and out of my body, so that I was looking down on the little girl who was being hurt from a safe distance. I felt that if me, the real me who lived inside, was out of my body, then no one could really hurt me by inflicting pain on my body. This coping mechanism was essential to my survival; however, as I grew older and the abuse ended, I continued to live in this detached way; it had become the only way I knew how to exist. It was all too easy for me to hurt my body as my father had done years before, because it was just my body, not really me.

In order to let go of Ed, I had to heal the rupture between my body and my self. This was frightening at first, because I felt so vulnerable. I will never forget the day I first gathered the courage to sit still for a few minutes touching my stomach (always the part of me I hated the most). I don't think I'd done more than brush past it before in my entire life, but now I sat and really let myself feel my tum and try to let go of all the fear and revulsion.

Slowly, I began to accept, appreciate and even love this body of mine that I'd hated for so long. I stepped back inside my skin and began enjoying the sensations of life once more. And when you're ready, you'll do the same.

Being unfashionable (and happy about it)

You aren't alone in disliking the body you live in: in fact, you're simply following the cultural norm. Nowadays, it's fashionable to worry about your weight, diet, go to the gym and despair over lumps and bumps, curves and wobbly bits. In fact, if you're not on a mission to change your body, you're something of an oddity to many: just watch a waiter's eyebrows rocket when a woman orders a full-sugar cola.

Focusing on body is all the rage. Turn on the TV, pick up a magazine, visit a local gym or eavesdrop on women chatting in a café: you'll be bombarded by the message that in order to be popular, successful, acceptable and loveable you must strive for the "perfect body."

Our society is obsessed with faddy fashion. One minute space hoppers are the bees' knees, the next you're nobody if you're not bouncing up and down on a pogo stick. One minute you're think you look pretty dapper in pixie boots and a rah-rah skirt, the next you're kitted out in fluorescent cycling shorts and a T-shirt that changes color when you sweat. One minute you're hot if you're tall, tanned and toned, the next you're meant to adopt the skeletal, drug-addict, waif look.

Following the crowd is exhausting (and expensive) enough when it comes to keeping up with the latest trends in toys, clothes, music, design and so on. But it's getting downright ridiculous when it extends to changing your body size to suit the times.

Once you recognize that the "ideal" body shape is constantly changing, you begin to see how fickle our society's concept of beauty is. This is particularly the case for women. In the 17th century, the artist Rubens painted the women who were considered the height of beauty. His paintings are of buxom, curvaceous, cellulitey and, by today's standards, "overweight" ladies. In the 19th century, being curvy was a sign of wealth (having plenty to eat) and was thus attractive. In the early and mid-20th century, screen goddesses had hourglass figures with big chests, hips and bottoms and tiny waists. Then, as the years progressed, female role models got steadily slighter, and the curve often gave way to the pre-pubescent lollipop-stick body. And as The Body Shop's Love Your Body campaign of the late '90s pointed out, *There are three billion women who don't look like supermodels and only eight who do.*

Who knows what society will deem to be the ideal body shape in 10, 20, 30 years from now? But more importantly, who cares? Your body isn't a lump of clay you can pummel, carve and mold into whatever shape society tells you it should be.

Take clothes shopping, for example. Say you usually wear clothes that are sized as small. You go into a clothes shop, pick some small-sized jeans and go to try them on. But after five minutes struggling to do the top button up on the darned denim, you emerge from the changing room hot, cross and tearful. Rather than trying on the next size up (you don't want anything with a medium label, thanks very much), you leave the shop vowing to go on a diet. You don't even consider the possibility that a) the shop has mis-sized the jeans; or b) the clothing manufacturer has reduced the size of a standard small (yes, they do that).

A hundred years ago, we tailor-made clothes to fit our exact body size. Nowadays, we try to fit our body into the shape of mass-produced clothes, and when the clothes don't fit, we decide that there's something wrong with our bodies and we must change them. Put like that, it does sound a bit silly, doesn't it?

Pulling away from the crowd isn't easy, and we all succumb to society's pressures sometimes. But the more you can free yourself from the tyrannical ideals of the culture we live in, and accept that you're absolutely fine, beautiful and loveable just as you are, the happier you'll be.

Defining beauty

What is beauty? What makes someone beautiful?

Fat, thin, tall, short, big, small, young, old, black, white, able-bodied, disabled: anyone and everyone is beautiful. Beauty isn't about us all looking the same; beauty comes in all shapes and sizes.

Some people say that smooth skin is lovelier than wrinkled, that fat is ugly and thin is beautiful. Well, that's their opinion, but it's certainly not fact. Those who are keen to judge others' appearances and to divide bodies into good and bad, beautiful and ugly are unhappy in their own skins. They don't accept and love their bodies, and so are unable to accept and love others'. They don't truly understand what beauty is.

Beauty comes from within. When people look at you, they don't just see hair or limbs or skin. They look into your eyes and they see you, the you inside. I'm sure you can think of someone you know who's drop-dead gorgeous on the outside, but pretty ugly inside. They may have supermodel good looks, but they're spoilt, selfish and cruel, and that mars their beauty. And now I bet you can think of someone who's the exact opposite: not very attractive by society's standards, but a really lovely person on the inside and, therefore, beautiful in your eyes.

Ten years ago, I was very hung up on being beautiful. I got up early every morning and spent ages styling my hair, putting on make-up and carefully dressing my thin body in a stylish outfit. Since my recovery I have a rather different look. I'm not thin, I'm not groomed and I'm clueless about fashion. I wear clothes I feel comfortable in, rarely use make-up and feel quite happy just as I am. And you know what? Friends and family who've known me for years tell me I'm much more beautiful now than when I was obsessed with my looks. And I believe them. Ten years ago, when someone looked at me they saw a miserable, withdrawn girl who hated herself and her body: not exactly attractive. Nowadays, when someone looks in my eyes they see a happy, healthy woman who's at peace in her body. Now that's beautiful to see!

Think about how you define beauty, for yourself and for others. Consider who's beautiful to you, and why. Ask yourself what others may find beautiful in you. And then look at where you're directing your energy: into beautifying your outside or developing your inner beauty, your passion, your humor, your vitality, your humanity?

Letting go of the transformation myth

Society bombards you with the message that by changing your body you can be happier and more lovable. It's a pile of claptrap. Happiness is about watching the sunrise, paddling in the sea, cuddling a baby, laughing with a friend; it's not about having a toned physique, perfectly tweezed eyebrows or a glossy mane of hair. And people love you because of who you are, not how you look: your partner doesn't love you because your jeans have a "small" size label and you have abs of steel; they love you because you're funny and affectionate and inspiring.

I remember vividly the fantasy that inspired me to push off the top of the Ed slide and began my sharp descent into anorexia. I had arrived in America for a four-month university exchange, alone, depressed and overweight after months of binge eating. Lying in my bed that first hot summer's night, the story of the ugly duckling that became a beautiful swan popped into my head. I began picturing myself stepping back off the plane in London at Christmas, slim and beautiful. My family would be awed by my achievement in losing so much weight, and when I went back to university people would stop and stare as I walked into rooms, transfixed by how lovely I looked. Men would fall at my feet; friends would crowd round me. I'd be happy, so happy.

Fascinated by the idea that I could make this fantasy a reality, I opened the door and invited anorexia in. And over the following four months, I was indeed transformed. I went to America a soft, curvy UK size 18; I returned home a hard-bodied size 10. Now I had fulfilled my dream, everything would be better, wouldn't it?

But the reality turned out to be somewhat different to expectations. Yes, I was thin, but I still didn't feel beautiful: no matter how much weight I lost it wasn't enough, and I looked in the mirror and felt uglier than ever. Transforming my body hadn't made me happier; quite the opposite, in fact. I was deeply distressed and depressed, and was now hooked on Ed. People stopped and stared when I entered a room, but there was no admiration or approval in their looks, just horror and pity. And far from winning me friends, my rapidly thinning body repelled them. My body was bearing testament to my inner pain, and no one could pretend that this pale, gaunt girl wasting away before them was a beautiful swan.

The cultures we live in perpetuate the transformation myth. But that's just what it is: a myth. Changing your body won't miraculously solve the problems in your life or take away the pain inside. Your body is just your body. It's not the key to a life of happiness, and it's not something that wins you love or acceptance.

And anyway, who says ducklings are ugly and swans are beautiful? That's an opinion, not a fact. It's all a matter of perception. And whenever I head to the local duck pond with a loaf of bread, I can't help noticing that the ducklings are a lot happier, chirpier and friendlier than the bread-hogging, arrogant swans...

Taking a long, hard look at your ideal body

The image you have of yourself at a certain size or weight or physique may well be a fantasy that you will never, ever be able to make a reality. Because your ideal body, the thing you dream of and work towards, may be entirely unrealistic.

This is the era of the cult of the celebrity. There are more famous people than ever before, and image is everything. Many people dream of looking like their fashion and media icons. But the truth is, unless you've met a person in the flesh, you really have no idea what they truly look like!

You simply can't trust TV screens, computer screens and the pages of magazines to provide you with a realistic view of someone. In these days of computer wizardry, images of models and actors and celebrities are transformed. Clever lighting slims and hides wrinkles. Airbrushing smoothes skin and makes it flawless. Software slims, tones, firms, reduces or maximizes as required. A curvy, freckly redhead with a wobbly tum and knobbly knees can become a svelte, auburn-haired goddess with a concave stomach and long, elegant legs at the click of a mouse. As Cindy Crawford famously told *People* magazine in the '90s, "Even I don't look like Cindy Crawford in the morning."

And you can even fall into a trap of idolizing someone in your own life, and putting them up on a pedestal of perfection, without realizing that the person is just as human as you. Unbeknownst to me for a very long time, my own relationship with Ed was driven by a desire to be like the mother I lost in infancy, as a way of being close to her and making her proud. And in the only photo I had of my mother when I was a teenager and young adult, she's heart-achingly beautiful. It's a black and white shot, and she looks ever so mature and like a Hollywood movie star. She's flawless, and very slim. So I spent ten years gazing at this photo and trying to make my naturally curvy body resemble my mum's ever-so-slim one. And then one day an aunt pointed out to me that the photo I treasured had been taken when my mum was still at school, and that in her 20s she'd very much developed what we call the Wilson curves. And in that moment I realized I had been chasing a rainbow all these years: my ideal of beauty was completely unrealistic.

Think about who it is you admire and aspire to be like. Is it the person's looks you wish you could emulate? How realistic is your dream to look like that person? Instead, can you find other qualities that inspire you? For example, can you admire their ambition, their creativity, their generous nature, and work towards being more like them in that way?

Allowing yourself to be soft

What is fat and what is thin/toned? Fat is soft. Thin/toned is hard.

Why are people so revolted by being soft? Because psychologically that feels a lot more scary and vulnerable than being hard.

Here's an example. When I was pregnant with my son, my stomach swelled to astonishing proportions. Thanks to a medical condition, my body produced too much amniotic fluid, and my son had a lovely swimming pool to float about in. I was truly enormous! Yet at no point did I feel *fat*, in the sense we use the word, because up until my waters broke my bump was rock hard. Then, I gave birth to my son, and discovered that until my womb shrunk back to size I had the softest, wobbliest belly I could ever have imagined. And it was fascinating to see how my feelings towards my stomach instantly shifted. Overnight I went from proudly poking my bump out in maternity shirts to feeling rather repulsed by my decidedly squidgy belly and hiding it beneath baggy T-shirts. And then I did some thinking and realized I was being ridiculous! So what if my belly was soft? It didn't change who I was, and it was a lovely cushion for my baby son as he fed. And so what if having a soft belly made me appear more soft as a person? I was a mummy now. I should be soft!

Sadly, society sees people who have fat on their bodies as weak or soft, and people whose bodies are hard, wiry or toned as strong, capable, or hard. But really, this is all a pile of codswallop. Your physique is no reflection of who you are as a person. And in fact it takes a lot more strength to accept your body as it is meant to be, even if that means it's soft in places, than to spend a lifetime driving yourself towards an ideal physique of hardness.

Knowing that the mirror lies

When you have an eating disorder, you look in the mirror and see a fat, ugly person gazing back. But what you *think* you look like and what you *actually* look like are two completely separate things.

Studies show that if you have an eating disorder, you have a distorted view of your body. Let's say I take a photo of you standing upright against a wall and I black out your body so all you can see is a silhouette. I show you the picture along with several others of larger and smaller silhouettes, asking you to pick which image is yours. You're very unlikely to select the correct photo; instead, you'll pick a silhouette of someone who's quite a lot bigger than you. What does this exercise show? Well, whether you're underweight, of average weight or overweight, if you have an Ed you think you're bigger than you actually are.

When I look back on photos of me from when I was very ill, I'm astonished by how thin I was. Yet back then, I know that I didn't see myself as thin at all. I looked in the mirror and saw fat, fat, fat. I couldn't realize at all how slim I was. In fact, I often picked out clothes that were far too big while shopping and was bemused when they hung off me. And one memorable evening in a bar I spent a good ten minutes sidestepping back and forth and saying, "After you; no, after you," to my reflection in a mirror, such was my inability to recognize myself (okay, cocktails featured heavily in the prelude).

Being aware that your mind plays tricks with you over your body image helps you challenge some of your body hang-ups. Next time you look in the mirror, really look. Listen to what your mind says and let yourself question, ever so gently, whether it's telling you the whole truth.

And as you look in the mirror, remember this: reflections never show how you *really* look, because the image is reversed: left becomes right and right becomes left. So your reflection in a mirror, on a camera lens or on the surface of a pond is always a slight distortion of how you actually look. Don't believe me? Ask a friend to stand in front of a mirror and then look at their reflection. The face you know so well will look different in the mirror, probably crooked and less attractive. Now ask them to stand in front of another mirror and they'll probably look different again: fatter or thinner, wonkier or straighter. Mirrors really do lie, so don't put too much faith in them!

Thinking about your body through the ages

Ed tells women that thin is best. But is it? Right now, your idea of the "perfect" body shape may be thin, but was this always your ideal? And will it always be?

Think of yourself as a baby (digging out old photos helps). See your smooth, pink skin, rosebud mouth, minute nails on teeny ticklish toes. Notice your plump little arms, your tubby, milk-filled belly, your roly-poly folds. Do you look at that baby and wish she was thinner? Are you repulsed by the soft baby fat? Or do you accept that, when it comes to babies, a little fat is okay? Is this baby beautiful, just as she is?

Now picture yourself as a young girl of six or seven. Visualize the curves of your well-fed belly, your gappy grin and the rosy glow of your smooth, chubby cheeks. Do you look at that child and wish she was thinner? Are you repulsed by her natural curves? Or do you accept that, when it comes to children, a little fat is okay? Is this little girl beautiful, just as she is?

Next, imagine that you're nine months pregnant, your stomach hard and swollen, your breasts big and bouncing, your physique softened and feminine. Do you look at that mother-to-be and wish she was thinner? Are you repulsed by her pumpkin-shaped stomach, full of baby, her hot, heavy breasts, full of milk? Or do you accept that, when it comes to pregnant women, a little fat is okay? Is this woman beautiful, just as she is?

Finally, move forwards in time and see yourself as an old lady. Your toddler grandson is nestled in your lap, leaning against the cozy, comfy cushions of your soft stomach and breasts. He puts his arms around your neck and nuzzles in to hug you, feeling your strong, warm, cuddly embrace. Do you look at that old lady and wish she was thinner? Are you repulsed by her plump figure, her rounded curves? Or do you accept that, when it comes to grannies, a little fat is okay? Is this woman beautiful, just as she is?

This exercise proved to be a real eye-opener for me. After years of hating my body, I was startled to find that I didn't feel any repulsion or dislike towards my young body. In fact, I rather liked the body I had as a child, and was perfectly happy to accept that the chubby little baby me grinning cheerfully in photos was pretty darn cute. Then, because I'd always wanted children (and hopefully grandchildren some day), I started thinking about how I wanted to look in the future. And lo and behold, thin didn't fit with that picture, either. I didn't want to be a diet-obsessed, skeletal mum or a frail, bony granny. I wanted to feel soft, nurturing and feminine; I wanted my children to see my body as warm, comforting and cuddly; I wanted to be a good role model so that they'd grow up happy in their own skins.

And then came my *Eureka!* moment. If it was alright not to be thin when I was a baby, a child, a mum or a granny, why wasn't it okay right now? Saying that it was okay to have a little fat on me at some stages of my life but not others sounded a bit bonkers, even to me. What if the beauty ideal I was trying to live up to was just a big con, a load of nonsense? What if it was okay to have the odd ounce of fat? What if that didn't make me ugly or a failure or unlovable? What if I just let go of needing to be thin, full stop? What if I just focused on being me-sized?

Ask yourself this: would your world end if you let go of your quest for thinness?

Accepting your body's natural shape

Your body has a natural shape and size: a set point at which it's happiest. Try as you might to fight nature, there's really nothing you can do about it. You can bully your body into being a different size and shape, but you'll always encounter resistance.

Picture a spring. Left alone, with no forces acting upon it, a spring remains the same shape and size. But what happens when you squeeze or stretch the spring? The spring will always try to return to its relaxed, natural form. You have to maintain constant pressure to stop it springing back into shape.

Here's how the body spring works in action:

- Squeeze the spring and it strives to expand again. The less you weigh, the harder it is to lose weight. Your metabolism slows, and you burn off calories less effectively. You have to eat less and less to achieve a weight loss that progresses at a limping pace. Your body wants to gain weight and return to its set point.
- Stretch the spring and it tries to shrink again. The more you weigh, the easier it is to lose weight. Your metabolism is faster, so you don't have to reduce your food intake much to see weight come off, sometimes at an impressive rate. Your body wants to lose weight and return to its set point.
- Leave the spring alone and it's happy. When you're at your natural weight, your body plateaus out. You have to really overeat to gain weight, and really under-eat to lose weight. Your body works to maintain balance. Your body is happy at its set point.

Recovery means letting your body settle at its natural shape. Everybody's natural shape is different: you may be naturally slim or naturally curvy, and either is just fine, if your body's happy. Remember, also, that your natural shape changes over time: as we age our bodies naturally change, and that's okay too.

Do a little detective work to discover your natural shape. Think how your body looked before your eating disorder, and how it responds now to weight loss/gain. You probably have a pretty good idea of what your body would look like if you allowed it to settle. Feelings of fear and revulsion may come up. Ask yourself what's holding you back from working with rather than against your body?

One day, when you're ready, you can accept and even like your body as it is. And when you leave that spring alone, you'll find it's not just your body that's relaxed and happy and in balance, it's the you inside as well.

Appreciating your body

Do you take your body for granted? Do you really appreciate just how intricate and clever your body is, and how much it does for you?

Think about all the things your body lets you do:

- Cry salty, purging tears
- Dance, swim, run, twirl, jump, stretch, lift
- For women, conceive, carry and feed a baby
- For men, make sperm to create a son or daughter
- Hear birdsong, waves lapping on a beach, a child's giggle
- Kiss and caress, and feel a lover's touch
- See rainbows, sunsets, stars, smiles, snow
- Sing, shout, hum, laugh, talk, share
- Smell autumnal bonfires, freshly mown grass, calming lavender

Imagine you woke up tomorrow deaf, dumb, blind and paralyzed; you'd be devastated. Your body gives you so much, helps you experience so much, lets you *live*.

When I look back at the years I hated my body, I feel sad. My poor body was starved, stuffed, purged, beaten-up, cut, poisoned and pushed to the absolute limits. I ignored all my body's anguished cries for help: the terrible hunger pangs; the pains in my stomach, my throat, my chest, my head; the muscles screaming in agony and exhaustion. I bullied and abused my body to the extreme, and it would have had every right to simply shut down and refuse to take my punishments.

And yet my body has been wonderfully forgiving. It took time to heal the damage I'd inflicted, but, years later, I'm blessed not to be carrying around the baggage of Ed any longer. I'm so grateful that my body has allowed me to let go and be happy and well, that it survived my terrible, hurtful abuse to go on and thrive and grow and glow.

Can you appreciate how much your body does for you, how unique and awesome and miraculous it is? Can you recognize that you don't always treat your body with the care and attention it deserves, that sometimes you take it for granted, that sometimes you hurt it? Are you ready to ask your body to forgive you? Are you ready to celebrate everything that's great about your body, to value the experiences it gives you?

Learning to trust your body

Ed tells you that your body is your enemy: dangerous, unreliable, untrustworthy. Consequently, you've taken control of your body and, irrespective of what your body says, you now dictate exactly what, when and how much you eat.

But what would happen if you gave the control back to your body, if you let your body guide you in your eating? The answer is: your body would guide you to eat happily and healthily.

When you listen and respond to your body's signals:

- You eat when you're hungry.
- You eat what your body wants.
- You stop eating when you're full.

Children are the best example of this kind of natural, intuitive eating. A baby will drink as much milk as he wants from the breast or bottle: he can't be coaxed to have more than he wants, nor will he accept having less (oh my baby son's outrage when he'd sucked his bottle dry!). A toddler in her highchair will demand food when she's hungry, select the foods she wants to eat on her plate and refuse a single mouthful more once she's full. She has a simple, trusting relationship with her body: her body tells her what it needs and she responds.

Research involving small children has shown that they are remarkably good at eating a balanced diet, even if it seems they aren't. Imagine you lay out a table full of lots of different types of food and for a week allow a child to choose their own food entirely. Although the child may eat a little strangely according to expectations (for example, eat two bagels for breakfast and then dip a pear in some soup for tea), over time research proves the child eats a healthy, balanced diet because they're in tune with their body.

So it's worth remembering that, no matter how long you've struggled with Ed, once upon a time you did have the ability to eat according to your body's signals: when you were a baby and young child. You aren't learning a new skill; you're merely remembering a way of eating you used to naturally follow.

Getting in touch with your body can be hard when you've ignored its signals for so long, but slowly you can rebuild the relationship. Here are some steps you can take:

- When you start thinking about eating, ask yourself what's hungry, your body or your heart? By eating, are you listening and responding to your body's signals or are you trying to manage some emotions?
- When you feel hungry, stop and really feel the sensation. Where do you feel the hunger: your throat, chest, stomach? What does it feel like: an ache, a growling, an emptiness? Close your eyes and ask your body what it's hungry for, what tastes do you want in your mouth?
- Experiment with feeling full. How quickly does your body signal that it's had enough? What does the signal feel like?

How full is too full? Do some foods fill you up more than others?

- Work on enjoying food. Take a slice of melon (or another food you feel safe with) and eat it very slowly. Place a piece of melon in your mouth and suck it. Taste the juice and feel it sliding down your throat. Next bite into a melon chunk, and feel the texture and the sensation of chewing. Really enjoy the flavor. After each mouthful, pause and ask yourself if you're still enjoying the melon. Do you want more? Do you need more? Once you decide you've had enough, move on and do something else, then later in the day remember how the melon tasted. Did you enjoy it? Are you still enjoying it?

Learning to trust your body takes time, so take it one step at a time and forgive yourself instantly when you aren't able to eat according to your body's signals. There's no perfection in recovery, and even when you've build that trust, there will still be plenty of times when you eat according to your mind's, rather than your body's, desires. That's okay, that's normal, that's fine. Sometimes I listen carefully to my body and eat salads and pasta and brown bread, and sometimes I indulge in ice cream or extra cheesy pizza, knowing that my body will crave something healthier later that will even my diet out.

With trust comes balance, freedom and calmness. The day will come when you slowly savor each mouthful of a slice of gooey, rich chocolate fudge cake, with complete enjoyment and no guilt. Oh, what bliss!

Responding to your natural rhythms

We all have natural body rhythms. When you respect these rhythms and go with them, your body is happy and so is your mind. But when you battle against these natural rhythms, you become slower, sluggish and depressed.

Consider these body rhythms:

- Seasonal: Many people who struggle with Ed also suffer from some degree of Seasonal Affective Disorder (SAD). This means you feel happier, more hopeful and more energetic in the lighter, warmer months, and down, negative and tired in the cold, dark ones. Because you're happier in spring and summer, your Ed symptoms are often less severe at that time, but in autumn and winter the balance shifts.
- Monthly: For women who menstruate, the cycle can majorly affect emotions and energy levels, and consequently Ed. You may notice you struggle more during ovulation and menstruation than at other times of the month.
- Daily: Are you up with the larks or a night owl? Some people find themselves in a better mood in the mornings, and full of energy and zest for life, but by evening they're exhausted and prone to Ed behaviors. For others mornings are hell, and the day gets progressively easier. And some find the day moves through a series of peaks and troughs.

Whatever your body rhythms, it's useful to be aware of them so you know when your body needs rest and gentle support. For example, say it's 8pm and you're feeling down, pessimistic and worn out, and you're considering a binge to dull the feelings. But is a load of food what your body really needs? Your body's trying to tell you something: that it's tired. An early night will be healing.

Over the years I've realized that my body likes spring/summer and is most energetic in the mornings. So on a winter's evening, I know that I'm much more likely to feel blue and lethargic, and like a hibernating bear I'll eat more at that time. That's okay. I accept this is my body's rhythm and I go with it.

Recovery is about understanding that nothing is constant. You won't feel the same way every year, every month, every day, every hour. And you won't eat the same way either. It's okay to accept that at different times your body wants different things. You can just sit back and let your body take charge.

Focusing on a new body target

Over the course of your Ed, your focus has likely been weight loss. Whether you have binge eating disorder, bulimia, anorexia or any other form of Ed, the ultimate fantasy in life is to be thinner.

Letting go of your desire to be thinner leaves a big void inside. If you let go of the drive to lose weight, then what will you work towards? You'll feel empty, unchallenged, lost.

You need a new direction, a new goal, and here it is: instead of trying to be thin, how about striving to be *healthy and strong*?

Being healthy and strong means:

- You're connected to your body and respond to its needs.
- You take care of your body and work with it, not against it.
- You let your body be its natural size.
- You do enough exercise to keep your body well.
- You give your body the foods it needs by eating a balanced diet (which, of course, includes some treats).

And the best thing about encouraging your body to be healthy and strong, rather than thin? Your body will thank you for your new focus. When you care for your body, it cares for you in return:

- You have more energy.
- Your health improves.
- Your hormones settle.
- You sleep better.

- Your appetite levels out.
- Your weight naturally stabilizes.

Being healthy and strong feels good, really good. Don't just take my word for it; give it a go. Start small, perhaps just trying to care for your body better for an hour at a time. And then, when you're ready, you'll let go of those damaging, joy-destroying goals and embrace a happy, healthy one that you can stick to for life.

10

Dealing with daily life as you heal

The journey from Ed to a place of healing takes a long time. And life doesn't stand still while you're doing the difficult work inside that helps you let go of your eating disorder: there's still so much to cope with, from work to shopping, eating out to falling in love. The following sections offer some practical tips on looking after yourself and minimizing Ed's impact on your daily life.

Caring for yourself
While you're tackling the painful and difficult reasons behind your Ed, you'll probably find, at times, that your behaviors become worse and make your life a misery. But perhaps you can find a way to lessen, however slightly, the debilitating, exhausting and painful impact your behaviors have on your daily life.

Here are some ways you can care for yourself just a little on a day-to-day basis:

- You may be able to pull back ever so slightly on the severity of a behavior. For example, if you have anorexia, perhaps you can allow yourself the tiniest amount of extra food: a few grapes, a cherry tomato, a slice of melon. If you have bulimia, perhaps you can stop purging a little sooner: when your stomach is empty, can you stop rather than continue retching? And if you're addicted to exercise, can you do just one less sit up or ten seconds less on the treadmill? Even the tiniest relaxation is a way of caring for yourself, without taking away the behavior that you need right now.

- If you're in the grip of anorexia or bulimia, your behaviors are no doubt physically exhausting you. Try to rest when you can: take a long hot bath, lie down and read a book, or have a nap.
- See whether you can find environments or circumstances that slightly improve your behaviors. For example, you may find it easier to eat something when you're alone or you may be less likely to panic when you cook your own food, rather than eating out. Whatever it is that makes you feel a bit safer, a bit calmer, go with it, and don't give a damn what anyone else thinks!
- If you need your Ed behaviors now, that's okay, but do you feel able to care for your body in other ways? For example, you may do some stretches, have an early night, drink plenty of water or rub some moisturizer into your skin. Even a simple, small gesture like swallowing a vitamin tablet is you connecting with your body and, on some level, trying to ease its pain.

Sometimes, you may find you take better care of yourself without necessarily planning to. For example, at the very end of my bulimia, when my body was desperately ill, I found myself binging on something comforting and very nutritious: jars of baby food. If you find yourself acting in an unusually caring way, don't panic and call the body-snatcher police. It's a really positive sign that you're beginning to heal.

Remember, getting better isn't about taking huge leaps forward. It happens in a series of teeny, tiny baby steps. Anything you do to care for yourself, no matter how small, is great progress.

Deciding who knows about Ed

On a daily basis you come into contact with many people: your family, friends, colleagues or classmates, shop assistants, bus drivers, the chap who comes to fix your leaky tap... The question is, who do you tell about Ed?

First and foremost, of course, you need to tell someone who can help you get the support you need, such as a doctor or a therapist. And you'll probably tell those closest to you when you're ready (if they haven't already worked it out for themselves): your partner, your parents, your siblings, your best friend.

But outside of your immediate support network, who needs to know about Ed? And who do you *want* to share your secret with? These are tough decisions. When trying to decide whether to tell someone about Ed, ask yourself the following:

- Why are you thinking about telling this person? Consider your motives: do you want their support, their sympathy, their attention? Do you want them to react in some way, perhaps do something to help you? Do you want to shock them or scare them? Do you want to help them understand what's going on inside you because they're worried or confused?

- How likely is it that this person will respond in the way you want? Can this person give you what you need? By preparing yourself for all possible reactions and considering how each would affect you, you're less likely to be floored by disappointment and hurt. The person you tell may give you exactly what you need, such as practical support. But they may also let you down and react with fear and ignorance. Check in with your intuition; you can probably sense how this person will react.

- Can this person keep what you say to themselves? Last but certainly not least comes confidentiality. If you tell this person, will they talk to someone else about your Ed? Will that friend gossip about you? Will that colleague go to your boss? Will that teacher have to report your problem (if your teacher is concerned that your Ed is life-threatening or that you are in a dangerous situation outside of school, they have a duty to tell a superior). Sometimes, you may be happy to tell someone in authority about your problem and allow that person to tell others who can help you. But you probably don't want to trust a friend, classmate or colleague with your secret only to find it's common knowledge the following day. Again, use your instincts to guide you on who you can trust. And before you open up, lay down the terms and check that this person agrees to keep what you say to themselves.

Also bear in mind that telling someone you have an eating disorder doesn't have to mean sharing your life story and the nitty-gritty of your pain, your struggle and your behaviors. You choose exactly how much you tell someone. For example, you may decide to explain that you have an eating disorder, but not the reasons behind it.

During your recovery, you may find that sometimes you're very open about Ed, and sometimes very closed, and that's normal and okay. When I first began sinking into anorexia, I definitely wanted no one on the planet to know what was going on. I was very, very secretive and exceedingly hostile to anyone who dared to comment about the changes in me. Then years later, when I was at my most ill, I was quite happy to shout my secret from the rooftops. I wanted the world to see me, to hear me, to know how much pain I was in. And I was determined to be defined by my illness. I was Pippa the Anorexic, Pippa the Bulimic, Pippa the Screw-up. Skip forward to today, and now I no longer feel the need to tell people about Ed. I'm not ashamed of it, and I will openly discuss my past if I want to, but I don't wear my eating disorder like a badge on my sleeve. Ed was and is a part of me, but I'm so much more than that as well.

Handling unwanted attention

When you have an eating disorder, other people's reactions can be hurtful.

Imagine you're in the cake aisle of the supermarket. You've been there some time, wavering between backing swiftly away and returning to the diet yoghurt aisle, or sweeping forbidden delights into your trolley and hot-footing it home for a monstrous binge. You're approaching complete meltdown when you spy a colleague from work, Emma, is standing further up the aisle, pretending to study a loaf of bread but sneaking looks at your flushed face and tearful eyes. You feel embarrassed, desperate and angry.

At work the next day you're in a toilet cubicle when you hear the door open and two pairs of feet click-clacking towards the mirrored area. A soft voice says, "Something wasn't right, Bev. She was almost crying right there in the shop. And she looked so thin and frail." Then a second voice brays, "Well, Emma, she's clearly got a screw loose. She never comes to lunch with us; she's a right loner. Silly cow. And what is she *wearing*? Baggy and black is so last year..." You sit silent and still, praying for them to leave. You feel lonely, ashamed and trapped.

People generally fall into two camps: those who are concerned and want to help, and those who gossip, judge and fear your Ed.

In this example, Emma may well be the former type: she saw you were upset in the supermarket, she's worried and she wants to help, but she's not sure how she can. Ignore people like this and they may just leave you alone. Alternatively, you may feel able to give a simple explanation so that the person understands what's going on and what they should do (generally, nothing at all).

Bev, on the other hand, doesn't sound like a candidate for Colleague of the Year. She's lacking empathy and sensitivity, and she misunderstood Emma's worried description as an invitation to bitch about you. She's ignorant and unkind, but underneath it all she's probably rather insecure about herself. How you deal with people like Bev is up to you. You may plaster on a huge smile and sail out of your cubicle, head held high, or you may come steaming out and give her what for. Either way, don't let her get to you. Who cares what she thinks? And as if you'd want to eat lunch with *her*!

Finally, with people like Emma and Bev about, it's easy to become a bit paranoid and convinced that others are watching you, analyzing you and judging you. But try not fall into the trap of jumping to conclusions. For example, you notice the chap opposite on the train is gawping at you, which makes you feel uncomfortable and squirmy. He's clearly horrified by your too-thin arms or disgusted by the amount of chocolate you've consumed in the last hour. But is he? No, actually he's unable to tear his eyes away because he fancies you. Creepy, but flattering...

Avoiding triggers

While you're healing from your eating disorder (and even once you've let go of Ed), it's wise to avoid things that trigger low self-esteem and Ed behaviors. Here are some things you may want to steer clear of in your day-to-day life.

- Celebrity nonsense: Some celebrities are perfection-seekers who spend bewildering amounts of time, energy and money trying to mold their bodies into what someone, somewhere has deemed beautiful. If looking at images of such celebrities makes you feel rubbish, remember that theirs is just one definition of beauty (and close up orange skin and glow-in-the-dark teeth are actually quite gruesome). In order to maintain their tiny, toned (or for the men, super muscled) physiques, the vast majority of these celebrities have pretty miserable existences centered on dieting and exercise, and many of them harbor secret Eds.

Are these role models for your recovery?

- Clingons: No, I'm not talking about *Star Trek* aliens, but about spending time with needy people who cling to you for dear life. Right now, you need to put you and your own problems first. You have enough to deal with without constantly getting burdened by cousin Janet's twice-daily rants about work or your mate Carl's tears and tantrums over his relationship break-up. I'm not suggesting you shouldn't be there for friends and loved ones by caring about them, listening to their problems and perhaps offering advice. But there's a big difference between a friend who chats to you about their problems and one who dumps them on you constantly and expects you to be a paragon of patience and understanding. If someone's clinging to you like a limpet on a rock, think about scraping them off and having a breather.

- Diets: Atkins, Cabbage Soup, GI, Bikini... there are hundreds of diets to choose from out there, many of which are depressing, limiting and decidedly triggering. To really get better you need to form a healthy relationship with food, and most of these diets don't help you do that at all. You're an expert on food and eating, and you know exactly what healthy eating is. Trust your own instincts with food and be wary of anyone who's written a book telling you the secret to happiness is to live off dried seaweed...

- Ed stories: You may find reading or listening to Ed stories triggers behaviors. I once bought a biography written by a girl who had anorexia, hoping that her recovery story would inspire me. Inspire me it certainly did, but not quite in the intended manner. I got lost in the lengthy account of her Ed behaviors, learned some new tricks and embraced them as my own. I put down the book, trotted off and got more ill than ever. My advice is to stick to uplifting stories, and skip any bits that may trigger behaviors.

- Fashion and lifestyle magazines: There are very few magazines out there that don't contain potential triggers. They're jammed full of diets, exercise plans, image-transformation tales (usually involving weight loss), "beauty" direction, images that vilify any celebrity who dares to look less than perfect and countless ads for products that promise to beautify, slim and tone. And even if the magazine does include an article entitled, "You're beautiful as you are," it's bound to be accompanied by images of wafer-thin, preened models and an ad for cosmetic surgery. Read with caution or avoid entirely and stick to uplifting reading matter.

- Food-/body-obsessed people: They're everywhere: in your family, down the pub, at work, in the post office queue... people who are utterly fixated on their latest diet, their weight, their clothes size, their new exercise program, their body worries. When you're recovered, you may feel able to chat happily to such people without their obsession affecting you. But when you're still healing, you have enough on your plate (pardon the pun), so don't get drawn into chatting about cellulite-smoothing lunges or that Chinese tea that makes you lose ten kilos overnight (yeah, right).

- Gyms: Years ago, I was a gym addict. I loved pushing my body harder, ignoring the aches and complaints, and building up time on the cardio machines and kilos on the weights. For me, getting better meant treating my addiction by quitting the gym for good. If you think the gym environment is a trigger for you, save yourself the membership fee and do something else to look after your body's fitness. A daily walk, a swim, a bike ride, gardening, buffalo lassoing... exercise should be fun, so do something you enjoy.

- Other Ed sufferers: Some people find friendships with other Ed sufferers a comfort during recovery, because they don't feel alone. But for others, contact with other Ed sufferers can trigger behaviors, because boy are we a competitive bunch! Imagine you're making progress with your Ed, but then you meet up with a friend who, sadly, isn't doing as well as you. She's very thin and frail, but she's firmly telling you she's in control of her life, her body and her feelings. Before you know it, Ed rears its ugly head. You look at her and feel fat in comparison, and you want to feel controlled and powerful like she seems to be. It becomes a real struggle not to slide back into destructive behaviors. So remember, if contact with other Ed sufferers has a detrimental effect on your progress, it's okay to pull back for a while.

- Skinny Minnie clothes shops: When you have an Ed, clothes shopping can be a real ordeal. It doesn't matter what size you are, you're bound to end up looking in a huge mirror lit by fluorescent lights and feeling depressed by the figure staring glumly back at you. Try to stick to clothes shops that make you feel comfortable: shops that aren't too busy and have natural lighting, private changing rooms, friendly assistants and realistic sizes. If it's all too much, try catalogue or Internet shopping for now, so you can try things on in the comfort and privacy of your own home.

- TV brainwashing: I could write an entire book deploring the negative messages we receive from our screens: actors who look like they've been cloned from Barbie and Ken dolls; adverts that tell us we need to lose weight to be happy and beautiful; makeover shows that tell people they must "transform" how they look because they're fat, ugly, old and frumpy; and programs that tell us what we "must" eat hosted by presenters who look, let's face it, gaunt, shriveled and ill. Notice how your viewing habits affect how you feel and behave, and be discerning about what you watch. Step back from the TV and think about what you're seeing. Try to separate reality from the fantasy world on screen.

- Weighing scales: Once you're within a healthy weight range and you've stabilized there, you may feel that you don't need to know exactly what you weigh anymore. I weighed myself several times a day for many years, but when I recovered I made a decision to smash my scales (really therapeutic), then there's no temptation to get obsessive about numbers once more. Nowadays, I go purely on how my clothes fit and I let a doctor weigh me once in a blue moon if it's essential. Letting go of the scales may be something you only do once recovered, but if you find yourself eyeing that sledgehammer, go for it, I say.

Managing work or study

Most Ed sufferers find it difficult to manage a job or studies while they're ill and recovering. Ed is exhausting and debilitating, and it consumes huge amounts of your time and energy. It can be very, very difficult to focus on work when you have so much going on inside, and to care at all about that report for your boss or the essay that's due tomorrow when you feel like your life is falling apart.

Here are some ideas that may help:

- Dealing with triggers: Places of learning or work can be minefields for Ed sufferers. At school or university you may struggle to eat with classmates in the canteen, to resist the call of the vending machines or to cope with group exercise sessions (think gym class in skimpy shorts). At work people's birthday cakes may be your undoing or you may find yourself wrestling with Ed during Friday's lunchtime pub session. Recognize that these are difficult, pressurized situations for you. Do what you can to avoid triggers or find tricks to minimize their impacts. For example, bring a packed lunch full of safe foods and leave your money at home, then you can eat in the canteen without it precipitating a binge.

- Telling someone: If Ed is affecting your studies or working life, confiding in a teacher or colleague may help you get the support you need to feel able to continue. But this is a big decision, so think carefully before telling anyone. See the earlier section on deciding who knows about Ed.

- Giving yourself a break: It's okay to take time out during your day if Ed is overwhelming you. Going to the toilet is often the best escape: once there, do some deep breathing, cry, close your eyes: whatever you need to do to feel better. Fresh air and a change of scene can also be very calming and re-energizing. Take a break at lunchtime and go for a walk, browse the shops or sit in a park. Get away from the environment that's making you feel trapped and panicked, and unable to express how you're feeling.

- Taking time off: Sometimes it all gets too much and you need distance from work or your studies for a while. At school or college, you may need to negotiate a period of leave; perhaps you can study at home for a while. At work you choose between taking holiday or sick leave, or quitting entirely. Whatever you decide, don't beat yourself up because you're taking time off. You aren't a superhero and you can't successfully balance work/study and an eating disorder all the time.

- Considering a change: If you're really struggling with studies or work it may not be just because you have an eating disorder. Think carefully about what's making you so unhappy. Perhaps you're not enjoying your course at university, you hate your school and are being bullied, or you're bored in your job and can't bear your boss. Can you change courses, schools, jobs? You may decide that sticking it out is the best option for now or you may realize that making a change would lift a big weight off your shoulders. Whatever you decide to do, no matter how mad it may seem to others or how inconvenient it is, if it feels right then go for it.

However difficult studying or working comes, don't despair. You're not alone: every other Ed sufferer is going through the same thing.

During my illness, I struggled immensely to handle work. At university, I lost interest in my studies and regularly skipped lectures and tutorials. I had to force myself to study, to write essays, to sit exams, to crawl through the remainder of my degree. It all seemed so trivial compared with the hell of my Ed and the severity of my pain. I hated the normality of university life, and I was deeply jealous of the students around me who, I was convinced, were living happy, carefree lives, free from depression, destructive behaviors and self-hate.

Following university, I battled through three jobs, clawing my way through the day. I was bored and unchallenged, and felt trapped and isolated. I always began a new job determined to tell no one about my Ed, and I would work hard to protect my secret: acting happy and positive when I felt anything but; glossing over the truths of my life, my past and my activities; covertly starving, binging and purging in the office, and covering my tracks with lies and pretence. Eventually, the pressure would become too much and Ed would be revealed, either because I desperately wanted support so I told someone, or because my body took over and let the cat out of the bag by making me simply incapable of working. Then I would feel increasingly uncomfortable in my job, sure that others were judging me, and would take more and more sick leave. Eventually, I would quit and move to a new job, starting the whole process once more.

After years of struggling to maintain a normal lifestyle, I finally made the difficult decision to take some time out. Despite the fact I was already in debt and had no idea how I would afford to live with no job, I knew I couldn't carry on working. Work simply didn't matter now: there was a time bomb inside me ticking louder by the second. I was slowly dying.

I took eight months off work, and spent my time going to intensive counseling. They were long, hard, dark months. I was lonely, isolated and in agony as I spent all day, every day battling Ed. But finally, I began to notice changes in me and in my Ed behaviors. I felt able to go back to work, but I decided I needed a complete change. So in the space of a year, I went from being a city PR girl to a nanny. I played on swings, I sang lullabies, I finger-painted, I watched *The Muppet Show*. Nannying was never going to be a permanent job for me, but I allowed myself to stop worrying about my future career and instead do something fun, inspiring, healing and manageable as I recovered.

Be prepared to make changes and to relieve the pressure on yourself by taking time out. And most importantly, don't beat yourself up if you're struggling to cope at work or at your place of learning. Getting up in the morning and dragging yourself to school or work is hard enough for anyone, let alone having to sit with Ed during that oh-so tedious team meeting or lecture on usage of the semi-colon.

Socializing

No man or woman is an island: we all need to be with people sometimes. Spending time with friends is great for recovery: you have fun, you learn new things and you see life from different perspectives. You step outside of your insular Ed world and connect with the people around you. While laughing, listening, chatting and relating, you forget about your problems for a moment.

But socializing can also be problematic when you're recovering from Ed. Here are some things that can interfere with you having a happy, rewarding social life, and ideas for tackling them:

- Eating out: This one's a biggie. Nothing reduces you to a shuddering, panic-stricken heap on the floor quicker than the words, "Let's eat out." You can't control calories, ingredients or portions sizes, you may be worried you'll binge, and you really don't want to wrestle with your demons in public, with other people looking at your plate and scrutinizing how much you've eaten or not eaten. Nightmare! You have two choices. You can go out to dinner and find a way to get through the meal, perhaps by picking the restaurant yourself, ordering safe foods (the kitchen is perfectly capable of making you a simple salad with no dressing, even if it's not on the menu) and having a ready excuse for any behaviors, such as a stomach upset. Alternatively, you can politely but firmly decline eating out, and either suggest an outing to a non-foody establishment or eating in (where you're in charge).
- Meeting new people: Ed goes hand in hand with low self-confidence, so you may find that talking to someone you don't know is an ordeal. My advice is to be gentle with yourself. Don't set high expectations and tell yourself you must be the most vivacious, friendly person at a party, and don't beat yourself up if you avoid such situations or find yourself clinging to the one person you do know in a room of strangers. Confidence comes naturally in time as you heal. You can't force it.
- Making plans: A strange side effect of Ed can be an inability to stick to plans. When I was ill, I would often happily agree to meet a friend but then work myself up into a total panic in the days before our rendezvous.

Suddenly, what had felt like a fun meeting became something huge and indescribably terrifying. Sometimes I'd push past these feelings and make myself go out, and sometimes I'd give into the weight of the terror and cancel (often with a rather lame excuse), then breathe a sigh of relief as the pressure instantly dissipated. If this sounds familiar, don't panic about your panicking. This all ties into your need to be in control, and as you heal this problem will miraculously ease. In the meantime, consider telling your friends how you feel so that they can understand when you need to cancel.

- Feeling agoraphobic: Some Ed sufferers find crowded places frightening. There's so much noise and bustle, and people come too close and invade your personal space. You struggle to feel safe, and yearn for home. Do what you can to protect yourself from this fear. Go shopping and travel when it's quieter, if possible. Walk rather than take the crowded bus or train. Stick to the edges of busy places; sit in the corner of a cafe near a comforting, solid wall. Or if all else fails you can adopt a technique I recently saw someone employ on the London Underground: wear a giant inflatable ring around your middle, so no one can get too close (effective but rather attention-grabbing).

- Boozing and drug-taking: Anything that numbs your mind and distances you from your feelings is welcome when you have an eating disorder. Alcohol and drugs can make you forget your inhibitions, your pain and your Ed behaviors for a little while, which makes them mighty tempting. You're sick of being so controlled all the time; you want to hand the control over to a substance and let go. This is all perfectly understandable, but you know, deep down, that Ed and booze/drugs are a very dangerous combination. Under their influence you may lose all control. You're desperately unhappy inside and rather than helping you forget that, two bottles of wine can unleash your darkest demons. You can't exercise moderation and you take it too far. Before you know it you're doing crazy things you'll regret the next day: hooking up with strangers, smashing things in a rage, hurting your body, lashing out at others. As tempting as it may be to view the world through the bottom of a shot glass or psychedelic drug specs, try not to run away from yourself in this damaging way. If you slip up, forgive yourself and move on. But keep reminding yourself that the healthy, happy future you're working towards doesn't include trashing your body and placing yourself in danger.

Finally, if you're getting in a real tangle about social situations, don't be too hard on yourself. We all struggle sometimes. If you go out for dinner and panic because you've eaten too much, that's okay. Forgive yourself. If you go to a party, take one look at the crowd of strangers and leg it, so what? Let it go. Trust that, in time, all of these worries will pass. For now, just do your best to look after you.

Dealing with relationships

It can be difficult to keep a relationship going when you're ill. You're very wrapped up in yourself and your problems, you're needy and vulnerable, and you're not always able to give your partner the love, support and attention they need. And your partner is no doubt struggling with your Ed too: feeling frustrated, shut out, helpless, scared and worried. As much as you love each other, you may find yourself rowing and growing distant.

To keep your relationship healthy, you both need to listen to each other and understand what the other person needs. You need your partner to be patient, loving and supportive, and your partner needs exactly the same back from you. You need your partner to believe in you, and have faith that you can beat Ed. And you need to be able to trust your partner and believe that they want you to get well.

It's important to recognize that your partner is only human. As much as they may want to, they can't wave a magic wand and solve your problems. They can stand by you, hold you, listen to you, laugh with you, but they can't save you from Ed. Only you can do that. You aren't the damsel in distress who can be rescued by a knight in shining armor. You have your own journey to go on and, as hard as it is, your partner can't walk beside you each step of the way.

Often, partners become rather fixated on the symptomatic side of Ed, because your symptoms are something tangible that they feel they can help control. For example, I had partners over the years who would ask me what I weighed, what I'd eaten that day, how many times I'd binged, and so on. It's nice that a partner wants to help, but realistically, this focus on your symptoms isn't helpful at all, and it moves the dynamics of your relationship from equal partners to child/parent or patient/carer. So it's okay to tell your partner (politely) that they can help you much more effectively by listening, supporting, accepting and loving you.

Another common problem Ed sufferers encounter is that a partner unwittingly hinders rather than helps recovery. Your partner probably doesn't understand what you're going through, or the steps you must take to heal, and will sometimes put their foot right in it and say and do the wrong things. Your partner may be especially uncomfortable with you beginning to express feelings that you've been keeping locked up, and on the behavioral side you may realize that your partner's eating habits are affecting your own. For example, if Friday night curry blow-outs are a tradition in your relationship, you may start struggling with this if you're trying to get a grip on binge eating.

As with every aspect of relationships, there's no simple

answer to getting past problems. It comes down to knowing whether or not you truly love someone and want to be with them, and if you do then you have to find ways to get past issues. The root of most conflict and unhappiness for those struggling with Ed is their partner's lack of understanding of the illness. And often the simplest solution is to ask your partner to learn more about Ed, such as by reading a book like this one. You can then respect the fact that your partner has tried to see the world from your perspective, and from this place you can accept their (hopefully occasional) unhelpful behavior.

Sometimes, recovery involves letting go of your relationship entirely. You may need some time to yourself to really explore who you are, or you may feel that the relationship isn't right for you anymore. Perhaps you and your partner are on different paths or have become stuck in a rut. Or perhaps your partner is doing nothing for your self-esteem, and is undermining your recovery.

Breaking up is painful, and the idea of being alone again can be deeply frightening. But you'll get through it, one step at a time. And the day will come when you look back and see the path you followed, and understand what you learnt from the relationship and how it helped you grow.

Whatever position you're in—single, loved up or fighting to keep a struggling relationship going—remember that in order to heal your focus right now needs to be you. And it's worth remembering that if you can't love and accept yourself, you're not going to be able to truly love and accept anyone else. So work on improving your relationship with yourself for now, and you'll open yourself up to a more fulfilling love life.

Caring for young children

Many people with eating disorders spend some, perhaps a lot, of their time caring for children, either in their jobs or at home. As delightful as young children can be, they're also very hard work, and can easily trigger Ed behaviors.

First of all, children are tiring, and they push your emotional buttons over and over again. Put together exhaustion and emotion and you have a recipe for Ed behaviors. For example, the parent of a newborn baby may get by on as little as a couple of hours' sleep a night, and staggers about in a haze of exhaustion. The baby cries and cries, which makes the parent either want to cry themselves, or shout, scream or run for the hills. In such a fog of despair, Ed may seem a pretty appealing solution.

Another problem is the focus on food, particularly with babies and toddlers. From weaning onwards you can find yourself agonizing about what your child eats, when and how much. Not only do you prepare your own breakfast, lunch and dinner, but you now have to prepare your kid's meals too, and they don't always coincide with adult mealtimes. Some days you feel you've spent most of the day preparing food, helping kids eat it and then clearing away. The level of contact with food is very difficult to manage, and can feel like torture if you're trying not to eat, or not to eat too much.

And then there's the little one's approach to eating. Your toddler doesn't just want to eat what's on her plate; she wants to eat half of your lunch too. And she wants to feed you part of her lunch, which you really don't want. You can feel like control over your eating has gone out the window!

Here are some tips to help you manage caring for children and caring for yourself at the same time:

- Take time out whenever you need. Put your child somewhere they're safe, and leave the room. Make a cuppa, take some deep breaths, try to relax and find some perspective.
- Although you need to keep a level of control over your feelings around kids, that doesn't mean you must lock

away all feelings. It's okay to cry a bit if you feel sad, or express that you're cross sometimes (note I say cross, not furious; children will be scared by you screaming at them in an out-of-control manner).

- If you're struggling to control your feelings, and you don't want to express them right now, allow yourself to be a bit detached from your kids for a while. If your toddler's clamoring for you to do a jigsaw with him, it's okay to ignore him for ten minutes if it helps you calm down and get control. The jigsaw can wait, and you won't scar your child for life by saying, "No, darling. Mummy needs a minute to herself."

- Forgive yourself if you struggle with eating behaviors around your kids. For example, if you find yourself binging on leftovers off your kids' plates that you don't really want or need, that's okay. Don't hate yourself and think you're weak. It's hard right now, but you won't always struggle like this. In time you'll lose the urge to binge (and one day your kids will be ravenous teenagers and there'll be no leftovers anyway!).

- Shield your children from Ed. Don't let your children realize that you're bingeing, purging or starving.

As I mention in Chapter 8, sometimes the children of people who have eating disorders follow in their parents' footsteps. Eating disorders often run in families. And these days children as young as four or five can show signs of an eating disorder. Here are some warning signs to look out for in a child that may indicate the beginning on an eating problem and/or poor body image:

- Asking about calories/fat content in food
- Avoiding mirrors
- Comparing their body size to other children's
- Eating robotically, seemingly without relating to the

process
- Eating secretively
- Exercising to lose weight
- Looking in the mirror often
- Refusing meals
- Requesting and eating lots of junk food
- Significant weight gain or loss
- Stealing food
- Using weighing scales
- Using words like *fat* and *ugly* to describe themselves
- Worrying about their size
- Worrying about the fit of clothes; choosing baggy clothes

If you suspect your child is beginning down the path to Ed, you need to talk to your child, listen to their concerns and give them reassurance. If you're concerned about their behavior or attitude, see a doctor. The quicker you catch Ed in a child, the less time the child suffers.

Realizing that your child is struggling with Ed isn't easy at all, and you'll no doubt be quick to blame yourself for passing Ed on. Try not to devote energy to self-blame: it doesn't help you and it doesn't help your child. Focus instead on what you can do right now to help your child heal. And don't forget that it may not only be your child who needs help: the more you can let go of Ed, the easier it is for your child to do so as well.

11

Accepting support

Admitting that you need help and having the courage to accept it is tough. No doubt you'd like to heal from Ed in the same manner that you fell into it: quietly, secretly, away from prying eyes. But if you go it alone, you're very likely to struggle with your recovery. Ultimately, you need others' expertise, advice, concern, perspective and encouragement. This chapter takes you through the various support options available to you so that, informed and empowered, you can choose the help that best suits you.

Choosing to accept help

The problem with Ed is, it's all rather dramatic and life-threatening, and people react accordingly. You're silently screaming at the world, "Look at me! Look how screwed up I am! Look how desperately, dangerously ill I am. Look how little I weigh! Look how many times I throw up a day! Look at how ghastly I look! Look at me, dicing with death!" Loved ones (finally) begin to hear these messages and are plunged into helpless panic. They cart you off to doctors, consultants, therapists, psychologists, psychiatrists, psychoanalysts, nutritionists, acupuncturists, you name it, in the hope that they will cure you.

But help only works if you want to be helped. If you don't want to get better, you won't, no matter what Doctor Jolly prescribes or Counselor Joy suggests. If you're forced into getting help against your own instincts and wishes, you're not in control and are not taking responsibility for yourself. Only once you want to let of Ed can you take control of your recovery. *Getting* help doesn't help; *choosing to accept* help does.

Once you're ready to accept help from others, you can decide what kind of support feels right for you. Everyone's different, and everyone needs and prefers different types of support at different times. Only you know, at an instinctive level, what support best suits you. Trust yourself. If right now you want to read self-help materials and chat to a close friend about how you feel, that's fine. If you feel that talking to a therapist is right for you, great, go for it. There's no right or wrong answer.

Deep inside, you have the power to get well. If you want to get well, you can. But wanting to get well and actually getting well are two different things. Once you feel ready to start letting go of Ed, outside support helps you deal with the *how* of recovery. You *choose* to get better and so that you can reach that place of peace and self-acceptance you *choose* to accept help.

Getting support from family and friends

Family and friends can be a great source of comfort and support, because they care about you and your recovery. But beware: not only may your loved ones not be able to help you, they may actually make you feel worse.

First of all, remember that parents, siblings, partners and friends often desperately want to help. They look at you and see your pain, and they want to take that away. They are frightened by your illness and by the change in you, and they want a magic answer that will bring you back. Often, your loved ones understand very little about Ed—why you have it, what it is and how you recover—and in their haste to help you they can get it very wrong. Because they love you, they think they know you and know what's best for you, but sometimes they just don't. Their "help" can become more of a hindrance in your recovery, because it comes with such emotional baggage.

In addition, you have to consider the very likely possibility that your Ed may be closely related to the nature of your relationships with loved ones. Often, the cause of an eating disorders lies in a family's past—abuse, incest, neglect, for example—and your relationships with family members have all sorts of underlying issues. And while you are ill, your current relationships with people may not be healthy. For example, you may be dating someone who's controlling and cruel, because you feel that's all you deserve, or you may be best friends with someone who you dominate and bully, because you need to control and vent.

For me, Ed was very much tied up with the history of my family and our ongoing dynamic, and when I was ill my relationships with boyfriends and friends were often far from healthy. As much as my family and my boyfriends loved me and wanted me to get well, they were too close to the problem that was making me ill in the first place. And it was only by distancing myself from the people I loved most and turning to an impartial therapist for support that I was able to disentangle myself and begin to heal.

Only you can judge whether a loved one is helping you or hurting you. There are bound to be people you count as friends who can be there for you, to listen to you, to hold you, to make you smile. And then there will be people you struggle with, who make you feel hurt and even more alone.

You have the power to choose who you want to support you, and how. If someone isn't helping, it's okay to move away from them for now and find some space. And if someone is helping, it's okay to let them in. Your loved ones want to help you and you need to show them how best to do that.

Ditching the damagers

Getting support from other people can be a real help in your recovery. But it needs to be the right support, from the right people. Not everyone can help you get better. In fact, some people, unwittingly or otherwise, can do more damage than good in their efforts to help.

When you're battling Ed, people I like to call *damagers* trip over themselves to comment on your illness, your behaviors, your body and shove advice on how to beat Ed and be "normal" down your throat. These damagers know very, very little about how Ed and recovery works, and while their intentions may be noble (let's hope so), their words are often poison. Whoever coined the phrase "Sticks and stones may break my bones, but words will never hurt me" had a screw loose.

Here are the kinds of things damagers come out with:

- What you need is a good square meal.
- Why don't you just pull yourself together?
- Of course, you always were a bit on the podgy side...
- Oh, you should try the Atkins Diet.
- Have you gained weight?
- How will you attract a partner acting/looking like this?
- Stop making such a fuss and just eat it! You like gateau, don't you?
- You'll never believe it! I lost seven pounds this week...
- In my day, we ate what we were given and we did what our parents said. There was none of this nonsense.
- All women worry about their weight. I don't see what the fuss is about. You're perfectly normal.
- I've made you a three-course meal and I'm going to sit here with you until you finish every bite.
- You should be grateful for the food you have. There are starving children in Africa.
- You've just been sick, haven't you? How can you *do* that to yourself?
- Tell me, does my bum look big in this?

Ahhhhh! It's enough to make anyone with an Ed freak out, throw things and indulge in fantasies of committing grievous bodily harm: all perfectly natural, understandable responses.

If you come across a damager, distance yourself as fast as

possible. Your best bet is to either politely change the subject or physically move away from the person. Then, once you're in a place you feel safe, you can let the feelings come: shout, cry, rage, scream, laugh, whatever you need to do. Talk to a friend or your therapist. Get those feelings out.

Once you've expressed how you feel, then you can get some perspective and see the damager for who they really are: often not a malicious, evil so-and-so as you first thought, but an ignorant, insensitive, narrow-minded fool. Calmer now, you can hopefully forgive (or at least forget) the decidedly unhelpful words. Rather than letting them haunt you and hurt you, you can blow them away like the petals on a dandelion clock.

And you can protect yourself from that damager in the future. Depending on the circumstances, you may avoid the damager entirely or simply pay no heed whatsoever to their nonsense. Alternatively, you may decide to confront the damager and explain how their words affect you. This last course of action takes some real bravery and is best approached when you feel able to have a calm, adult conversation.

How you deal with a damager is entirely up to you. Just remember, no one has the power to hurt you unless you give them that power. Recognize damaging words, vent the feelings that emerge and then let go and move on. Life's too short.

Seeing a therapist

If you're ready and willing to work on what's behind your Ed, then counseling can be a real lifeline. The right therapist can help you fathom what's causing Ed, and guide you on your journey to recovery. They can create a safe place for you where you can truly be yourself and let those harrowing feelings come out into the open.

I use the term *therapist* to refer to anyone who offers talking therapy. A therapist in this sense may be any of a number of different professionals, often with bewildering and intimidating names beginning *psych–*. Different types of therapists work in different ways, depending on their training and experience: some may focus on your childhood; others may want to work on changing the way you think in order to transform your behavior.

If you're referred for free therapy through your doctor, you may not have any choice about what kind of counseling you have or who counsels you (although if you really can't see eye to eye with a therapist, you have the right to ask for a transfer). If you are able to afford private counseling, you have more options and can research types of therapist to see what form of therapy will suit you best.

For counseling to be effective, it's essential that you feel comfortable and safe with your therapist; after all, you'll be bearing the deepest, darkest parts of your soul to this person. You need to be able to trust your therapist, so that you can really take on board their suggestions and comments. And you need to feel that your therapist understands you, believes in you and doesn't judge you – whatever you may do or feel.

You may find that you work with several different therapists over the period of your illness and recovery, and perhaps even after you've recovered as well. Over the years, I've seen ten different therapists. Some I saw for just one session before I walked away, because I felt uncomfortable with the person or that it wasn't the right time for me to have counseling. But I stuck with other therapists for longer periods of time, from between eight weeks to two years.

Sometimes, you're lucky enough to find a therapist you really click with. My last therapist, Anna, was with me through the very darkest days of my Ed, and it was while working with her that I really faced the roots of my problems and began to turn my life around. A kind, gentle, motherly lady, she was exactly what I needed to heal. She made me feel safe; she seemed to under-stand exactly how I felt and what I needed; she gently pushed buttons that needed to be pushed; and no matter how bad I felt, she reassured me that I could live my dream of being healthy and at peace. I used to call her magical because I felt she weaved some kind of spell on me during sessions. But she would always laugh and tell me that the magic was all mine: the changes in me were all down to my own hard work and spirit.

In my experience, and for others I know who have struggled with depression and eating disorders, counseling really can make all the difference. If you feel ready and you can find a therapist you're comfortable with, give it a chance.

Taking medication

Sit in front of a doctor looking skeletal, or confessing that you go through 17 bags of chips a day and throw up hourly, and it's a safe bet that one of the first suggestions from your doctor will be medication. Most doctors and therapists recommend drugs as part of the treatment of an eating disorder. So if you're struggling with Ed and you seek help, you'll likely be faced with a choice of whether to go on tablets or not.

The thinking behind prescribing drugs like anti-depressants and tranquillizers is that these medications numb you. They reduce the hold of compulsive, regimented thoughts, panic and anxiety, depression and overwhelming feelings, and can therefore reduce corresponding behaviors like binging, purging, starving, self-harm and obsessive-compulsive disorder.

Medication can be very helpful in reducing the severity of your Ed. But drugs are not a magic cure. Be very wary of anyone who tells you that a pill can solve all your problems; it can't. Taking medication is a way to diminish some of Ed's strength, so that you can get some time out and really work on what's behind your eating disorder. Medication is not a stand-alone support system; it needs to work in conjunction with other types of support, such as counseling.

And medication is not to be taken lightly. All drugs have side effects, and medications such as antidepressants are no different.

You may feel dizzy or drowsy, and you may feel disconnected from the world and struggle to feel much at all sometimes. You need to work closely with your doctor to find the medication that best suits you, and to ensure your dosage is correct. And you must come off these tablets very slowly and gradually, as many commonly prescribed drugs cause unpleasant withdrawal symptoms.

Over the years, my doctors tried a range of medications before I settled on one type of antidepressant. Although I disliked taking the drug, I recognized that I needed the support it gave me as I tackled very painful issues with my therapist. Having avoided the terrible feelings I had inside for many, many years, the medication gave me the buffer I needed to start dealing with these feelings without being utterly overwhelmed by them. And once I moved on from counseling and began seeing a big improvement in myself and my Ed behaviors, I was able to come off the tablets gently over a period of months. Although it was very strange and a little scary to be fully "in the world" once more, without any medicated numbness, boy did it feel great too, because I was finally ready and able to experience all the feelings life brings: good and bad.

Taking medication is your choice. It's your body, and you choose what goes in it. Working with your doctor, you choose which medication you feel comfortable with, at what dosage and how long you want to take it. Listen to the advice of professionals working with you, and then make the choice that's right for you. Do what you need to do to feel okay inside, to get well.

Using self-help materials

The beauty of reading self-help material is the flexibility it affords. You can dip in and out of a self-help book whenever you fancy, whenever it feels right for you. You can find a book that speaks to you and makes you see things differently; you can pick bits out of different books and mix them together to find strategies and perspectives that work for you; and you can reject anything you dislike or disagree with. You're in charge, and there's no pressure to do anything you don't want to do.

There is a wealth of self-help material available, from books to websites. Some of them are really helpful; some are anything but.

Look for self-help materials that are:

- Creative: You want to look at Ed from different angles, and discover new ways to think about things. Creative, arty, fun ideas often have more impact than dreary clinical strategies.
- Empowering: Recovering from an Ed is about taking responsibility for yourself and making the right choices for you. Self-help materials need to make you feel you *can* get better, that the power to do so is within you.
- Informed: The best self-help materials are written by experienced and sensitive professionals or those who've *really* recovered from an eating disorder.
- Inspiring: You need to feel energized and excited about the message. The material needs to speak to you and make you think, "Hmm, interesting."
- Non-judgmental: A self-help book shouldn't make you feel any more isolated than you already do. You need reassurance that your problems are normal, under-standable and surmountable, and that you aren't a bad person for having an eating disorder.
- Practical: You need information you can apply in your own life, not airy-fairy irrelevant ramblings.

Steer clear of self-help materials that are:

- From a questionable source: Beware anything written by Mrs. Know-it-all, who's done a cheap online counseling course and thinks that equips her to advise on Eds, even though the closest she's ever come to an eating disorder is watching *The Karen Carpenter Story*. Likewise, watch out for self-help materials written by "recovered" sufferers who blatantly haven't recovered at all and are sadly still living with Ed.

- Negative, questionable or just plain wrong: If halfway through your self-help book you read, "You never recover from an eating disorder; you just learn to live with it," chuck that book in the nearest bin, burn it or encourage your three-year-old niece to use the pages for her latest crayon artwork.
- Obsessed with food: Remember, Eds aren't about food: that's the symptom, not the problem. So a book that sets out eating structures and food plans isn't very helpful. Besides, you don't need a book for that; you're the expert!
- Overly clinical: Don't bother with books that are dry, rigid and full of medical mumbo-jumbo. Do you really need a book that tries to pigeon-hole you as a textbook anorexic/bulimic/binge eater? Thought not.
- Pro-Ed: Some websites in particular contain advice that puts Ed in a positive light. Avoid like the plague!
- Rigid and prescriptive: The last thing you need is a book laying down laws and rules, and attempting to control your Ed for you.

Use whatever self-help materials work for you. Go with your instincts. If you like what a book is saying, great. If you don't, reject it or put it away for another day.

Trying complementary therapies

The clue is in the name: complementary therapies complement other support, such as counseling and self-help. They can help you really connect with your body, and focus on nurturing and healing it. They can alleviate side effects of Ed, such as digestive problems. And they can help you release feelings, and feel more relaxed and calm inside.

Here are some of the many complementary therapies you can try:

- Acupuncture
- Aromatherapy
- Color therapy
- Crystal healing
- Emotional Freedom Technique (EFT)
- Hypnotherapy
- Massage
- Meditation
- Reflexology
- Reiki
- Shiatsu (acupressure)

You may think that to benefit from these therapies you need to commit to a long-term course, but that's not necessarily the case. The immediate effects of a relaxing massage or reflexology treatment can extend into the following weeks, and the very fact that you are trying to nurture and heal your body at all is fantastic news for your long-term recovery. So if you can only do a complementary therapy once in a while, that's still a great step forward in your healing.

Unfortunately, these complementary therapies come at a price. If you can afford to do a therapy now and again, treat yourself. But remember you can also adopt a DIY approach for some therapies, such as massage, crystal healing and reflexology. Buy a book or just pay for one session with a therapist and ask them to show you some "do at home" exercises.

Knowing when to persevere, and when to quit
Whatever support you have, there are bound to be times when

you're screaming inside, "This is useless! It's not working! I've had enough. I quit!"

Sometimes, it's very hard to see how a particular type of support is helping you. Perhaps your therapist is pushing buttons that leaving you in agonizing pain, and Ed is worse than ever. Perhaps you've taken the tablets your doctor prescribed for a month now, but seen no improvement. Perhaps you've immersed yourself in complementary therapies, but still feel numb and disconnected from the world. You feel frustrated and let down, your confidence in the support dwindles and you feel hopeless once more.

But before you throw in the towel and sink back into despair, take a moment to check in with yourself and ask:

- Am I ready for this support? For example, if you're forcing yourself to go to counseling, but you really don't want to be there and don't want to take on board anything the therapist says, perhaps you need to take some time out. You can try again in a while or you may find a different sort of support that feels right for you at this point.
- Have I given this support a fair chance? Recovery takes time and it's incredibly painful, frustrating and exhausting. No support works overnight. As hard as it is, you need to have patience.
- Is this kind of support right for me? If your gut feeling says this support will help, if you give it time, then you need to find the strength to sit with these difficult feelings until they pass. But if your instincts are screaming, "This isn't right for me," then it's okay to review your support options and try something else.

During my recovery I spent countless hours questioning the support I had. Every time I saw my last therapist I would complain that the therapy wasn't working: in fact, the more counseling I did, the worse my behaviors got. Every time, she would smile at me and patiently explain that I was doing great, and that this "one step forwards, two steps back" pattern was a natural feature of recovery. I struggled against what she said but deep down I trusted her, so I kept going back to work with her again and again and again. And sure enough she was right: her therapy was a very important tool for my healing.

But I didn't always stick with support. A well-meaning friend once took me to her acupuncturist, telling me this "miracle man" would rebalance me and release the pain inside. I was very reluctant to go, but Nice Pippa was firmly in control and I didn't feel able to say no. Once on the bed, with needles sticking out of various parts of my body, I didn't feel good at all. I felt sore, vulnerable and overwhelmed by pain. No doubt the acupuncturist had done a superb job of bringing the pain to the surface so that it could wash away, but I simply wasn't in the right place inside to handle the feelings flooding through me. He removed the needles, I got dressed and I sobbed all the way home on the Tube, to the utter horror of the surrounding commuters. I never went back to the acupuncturist, and I accepted that this wasn't the right kind of support for me at that stage.

Whether you decide to persevere with support or run for the hills, be kind to yourself. Trust that whatever you choose to do is the right thing for you right now in your life.

Connecting to a higher power

There is one further type of support you can explore, if you're prepared to step out of the physical and into the spiritual.

Faith is a very personal thing. You may be an atheist and believe there is nothing in the universe outside what we can see and measure. That's absolutely fine; feel free to skip this section.

On the other hand, perhaps you believe that there's something in the universe that's bigger than us: a higher power. You may be religious and believe in a God; you may believe in angels, spirits, reincarnation or fate; or you may simply believe that there's something more out there than what you learn in science class, but not want to define it.

Faith in a higher power can be very comforting when recovering from Ed. Believing that there is a force out there watching over you, loving you, protecting you and believing in you can give you strength and support. It helps you feel less alone and more connected to the world.

Believing in something bigger than myself certainly played a part in my recovery. I'm not religious but during my recovery I developed many comforting beliefs. One of these was a faith that angels watch us: not in the sense of white frocks and giant wings, but that someone who has left you can stay close. When I look back over the years of my eating disorder, at the agony I used to feel and the awful things I used to do to myself, I know without doubt that my angel, my mum, was with me always, watching over me, loving me, protecting me and guiding me.

Perhaps such beliefs sound nutty to you; perhaps you believe something completely different. That's fine. Whatever you believe in is fine. But when you're down in that deep, dark hole, hurting, frightened, angry and so, so alone, look up. Perhaps there's a light coming from above you, and a hand reaching down to help you up.

12

Inspiring your healing

All sorts of things can speak to you during your recovery, from books to music, films to art. In this chapter, you'll find an eclectic mix of some of my favorites that may inspire, uplift, comfort, motivate and free you. I hope in time you can add plenty of your own.

Books

AA Milne, *When We Were Very Young*: Transport yourself back to a time when life was simple and charming, and especially embrace the stout and proud ted in "Teddy Bear."

Eric Carle, *The Very Hungry Caterpillar*: Remember this children's book about a caterpillar plowing through a lot of food and then transforming into a butterfly? A nice metaphor for your recovery.

Kaz Cooke, *Real Gorgeous*: A brilliant, funny, empowering book that promotes positive messages; an essential read for all women.

Kim McMillen, *When I Loved Myself Enough*: If you only read one book, make it this; it's recovery in a nutshell and gives you a warm, fuzzy, peaceful feeling inside.

Marcia Germaine Hutchinson, *200 Ways to Love the Body You Have*: Full of gentle, nurturing exercises that help you connect to your body.

Oriah Mountain Dreamer, *The Invitation*: Read this book when you're trying to face your pain; it's inspiring, comforting, and full of truth.

Rick Kausman, *Calm Eating:* Such simple words, and yet so powerful; a helpful guide to listening to your body and responding to its needs.

Susie Orbach, *Susie Orbach on Eating*: Similar to Kausman's guide, this concise book lays down the basics of getting in touch with your body and eating happily and calmly.

Music

Alanis Morissette, "Perfect": Nicely sums up the pressures of perfectionism.

Christina Aguilera, "Beautiful": For when you need to remember that you're gorgeous, just as you are.

Christina Aguilera, "The Voice Within": Connect with the nurturing, wise, guiding part of you.

Curtis Stigers, "(You Deserve) To Be Loved": Well, you do!

Dido, "Slide": One to put on when you're battling demons.

Labi Siffre, "Something Inside So Strong": Oh so uplifting and empowering.

New Radicals, "Don't Give Up (You Only Get What You Give)": The title says it all really; for when you need a kick up the butt.

Nina Simone, "Ain't Got No/I Got Life": A great song to help with connecting to, and appreciating, every little part of your body.

Nina Simone, "Here Comes the Sun": A soothing, comforting lullaby for when you're struggling to see the light.

Robbie Williams, "No Regrets": Make it your motto.

Sarah McLachlan, "Angel": For releasing pain and finding comfort.

The Beatles, "Let It Be": A song for letting go and finding acceptance.

Movies/TV

Amélie (2001): The kind of film that reinforces being who you are, and liking that person.

Bridget Jones's Diary (2001): There's too much focus on weight and looks for my liking, but she's a curvy heroine who's loved "just as she is".

City of Angels (1998): The idea of angels surrounding and comforting us is lovely, and the scene in which Meg Ryan takes her time to really savor a pear is thought-provoking.

Patch Adams (1998): If you can get past the cheese factor on this one, the message is rather poignant.

Shrek (2001): Who says green trolls aren't gorgeous?

Ugly Betty: She's successful, attractive and generally happy, but she sure as hell isn't skinny, groomed or dressed to impress: a good role model.

Art/photography

Beryl Cook: A British artist who painted comic, vivid pictures celebrating well-rounded people. Find out more at www.berylcook.org.

Spencer Tunick: An American artist who takes pictures of huge groups of naked people from a distance. His photos really challenge how you see the human body.

Yann Arthus-Bertrand: His Earth from the Air series of photographs is beautiful and gives you the feeling of being just one part of a whole picture of nature and humanity.

Websites

www.anitaroddick.com: Some great material on body image. Look out for the campaign posters of Ruby, the real woman's Barbie: curvaceous and beautiful.

www.any-body.org: Full of information, discussion and campaigning on changing cultural attitudes to body image and eating for women.

www.campaignforrealbeauty.com: The beauty product manufacturer's Campaign for Real Beauty site, full of inspiration, info and great resources (especially for young people).

www.iusedtobelieve.com: Just for fun; a site to help you get in touch with your inner child.

www.thebodyshop.co.uk: Their ethos, marketing and products are a breath of fresh air and promote good self-esteem and a positive body image.

Words of wisdom

"It's life that's too short, not your legs." – Body Shop campaign poster.

"Scales are for fish, not people." – Susie Orbach

"You don't have a soul. You are a soul. You have a body." – C.S. Lewis

"Understanding is the first step to acceptance, and only with acceptance can there be recovery." – JK Rowling

"Sometimes you have to let go to see if there was anything worth holding onto." – Anon

"Life loves the liver of it." – Maya Angelou

13

Understanding the true nature of recovery

No doubt you dedicate much time and energy to dreaming about life after Ed, and it's those dreams that guide and inspire you through your recovery. But how realistic is your vision of an Ed-free life? What is recovery and how does it feel? How can you tell that you're recovering and then recovered? This final chapter tells it like it is: what it's really like to let go of your eating disorder.

Knowing that complete recovery is possible
If you take away one thing from this book, make it this: it is possible to completely let go of an eating disorder.

During your illness and recovery, you'll no doubt read or hear some of the following:

- You never totally get over an eating disorder.
- You don't let go of an eating disorder, you learn to manage it.
- You'll always be very aware of your weight and what you eat.
- An eating disorder is something you have to accept and live with.
- Letting go of Ed entirely is an unrealistic goal.
- Ed is your crutch, and you'll probably return to it whenever things get tough in life.
- The best you can hope for is 90 percent recovery. There will always be times Ed rears its ugly head once more.

Attitudes like these are very, very damaging: they're negative, limiting, hope-destroying and, in my experience, only true for *some* people, *some* of the time. These are generalizations that don't have to apply to you.

When I came across messages like these, my instant reaction was belligerence: "How dare you tell me what I can and can't achieve? Who are you to tell me I can't find a way to free myself from this miserable eating disorder? You say that there'll never be a time I look in the mirror and like what I see, that I'll never be able to fully relax in my eating... well, screw you!" Never someone who liked being told what to do and what to be, I used these negative messages to motivate me in my recovery.

I'm living proof that you really can let go of Ed, and live a life free from the cage of control, restrictions and self-hate. You can sit by a lake, watching the sunlight dance on the ripples, and feel wonderfully, joyfully at peace with the world and yourself.

Defining recovery

Ed is all about being in control and being perfect. It makes sense, therefore, that letting go of Ed means letting go of being in control and being perfect. Simple, eh?

Well no, actually. If you're anything like I was, your thinking is very black and white. So while Ed is the epitome of all that's horrid, dark and bleak, recovery is a heaven of blue skies, warm sunshine and little white fluffy clouds. You may have an idealized picture of Ed recovery that looks something like this:

- When I'm better, I'll never overeat.
- When I'm better, I'll never under-eat.
- When I'm better, I'll never worry about my weight.
- When I'm better, I'll always be happy with my body.

This vision for recovery simply isn't unachievable (unless you're a robot), and by striving for this kind of perfection and control, you're actually still in the grips of Ed.

The true definition of recovery is having a normal, healthy relationship with food, eating and yourself. And guess what? Normal and healthy means being a human being who has strengths and weaknesses, successes and failures, ups and downs. So rather than that angelic, regimented recovery you may have expected, your true recovery looks like this:

- Some days you listen to your body and eat exactly what it needs, no more, no less. Other days you over or under-eat a bit. That's normal, and you accept it.
- Some days, you feel happy inside your own skin, and like what you see in the mirror. Other days you feel a bit less confident, and wonder if your ears poke out too much. That's normal, and you accept it.

Ultimately, recovery is about stepping out into the world and accepting your flaws and weaknesses. It's about loving yourself not in spite of your imperfections, but for them, because every little imperfect detail about you is what makes you human, just like everyone else around you. You don't need to control your journey, to rule it with an iron fist, to put pressure on yourself to perfect your recovery. Sit back, feel, experience, trust and accept, and then recovery will come to you: quietly, gently, wonderfully.

Accepting the possibility of relapse

When I was at my very worst with Ed, my fairy godmother (it's a long story) introduced me to Emily, who was a good way down the path to recovering from bulimia. Emily took one look at my thin, withdrawn, cowering form and told me her story. And as she spoke, my nerves gave way to excitement and my despair to hope. Here, sat before me, was someone who'd been where I was and had climbed out of the pit. Here was someone who used to starve, binge and purge but who no longer used these behaviors. Here was a girl offering proof that recovery from Ed is possible.

That day and Emily's words are forever etched in my memory, because they represented a real turning point for me. But one particular aspect of her recovery that she shared with me made more of difference than anything else. Here's how that part of the conversation went:

Me: You haven't had bulimia for two years now?

Emily: That's right.

Me: So that's it. You won't get ill again.

Emily: Whoa! Hold on there; I never said that. I can never say never.

Me: I don't understand. You've beaten Ed; it's over, right?

Emily: That's not how it works. Every day, I have to accept that one day, if I need to, I may go back to bulimia. If things got really tough, maybe I'd start vomiting again.

Me: But how is that recovery then? How can you live with that hanging over you?

Emily: It doesn't hang over me; it frees me. If I told myself I could never, ever use an Ed behavior again, that's very black and white, and it puts a lot of pressure on me. It means if I ever did slip up, it would be the end of the world. If I vomited just once, I know I'd get really ill again really quickly, because I'd beat myself up so much. But this way, I tell myself that if it happens, that's okay. I can just forgive myself for the bulimic behavior and then move on. It makes it less likely I'll binge and purge in the first place, because it's less of a big deal, and it makes the chances of a full-scale relapse much lower.

Me: So you accept that it's possible, and that if you binged and purged again you'd forgive yourself. But you still hope it never happens?

Emily: Of course; I never want to go back there. But I accept that if something awful happened, like someone I loved died, I may find it hard to cope, and bulimia may be the first thing I'd turn to. But because I've come so far in my recovery now, I think even if I went back to it, I wouldn't have bulimia for long. It would be a knee-jerk reaction, but I've done too much good work on myself to slip right back to the depths I used to be in.

Me: So you don't worry about relapsing?

Emily: Not really. The further you get in your recovery, the less worried you are. You know that you've been as low as you could be and got better, so you don't feel so scared about facing lows again.

That day, I put my faith in Emily's words and I began rethinking my approach to recovery. By accepting the possibility that I may relapse, but feeling that was okay and was something I could handle, I let go of a lot of the fear that had been holding me back from progressing.

As a point of interest, this turned out to be a conversation not about a hypothetical possibility, but a reality. Some years later, Emily hit a very tough patch and guess what? I picked up the phone one day to hear the dreaded words, "I've just binged and purged." I promptly put myself in complete panic mode, envisioning a painful, destructive relapse. But when I spoke to Emily a few days later and demanded to know how she was and what she was doing about her relapse, she laughed and said: "Relapse? Hell no! I only kept that up for a couple of days. It just doesn't work for me anymore. I found I couldn't really be bothered to keep eating or to throw up afterwards. I knew exactly what was behind the behavior, and all my old tricks had just lost their magic. Nah, bulimia just doesn't work for me now..."

Recognizing progress

Here are some basic facts about your journey to cut loose from Ed. Progress can be:

- Hard to see: Your behaviors are worse than ever and you're a seething mess of horrid feelings. You feel terrible: how can this be progress? Well, if you're starting to experience the feelings you've been blocking, you're bound to feel miserable and turn to Ed to cope. But each time you work on those feelings, you're taking a step down the road to recovery. When you look back with hindsight, you'll see just how much progress you made when you thought you were getting worse rather than better.
- Jerky: If you could make a graph that charted your progress, it certainly wouldn't show a smooth upward curve. Sometimes you nudge your foot forward a millimeter, and sometimes you take a big stride towards recovery. Sometimes you take a step forwards, then three backwards again.
- Slow: Recovery can be frustratingly slow. I can't give you an exact timescale, but I can promise that it won't happen overnight. Letting go of Ed takes as long as it takes.
- Different to expectations: Who knows what you'll discover on your path to letting go of Ed? Perhaps you think your recovery will see you a size-6 lawyer living in the city, but instead you become a size-14 florist living in the country. When you start to really get in touch with who you are and what you want, your recovery can take you to some surprising places!

If you're working on the things I highlight in this book—identifying the causes of Ed, getting in touch with your feelings, connecting to yourself and your body—then you're making progress. It doesn't matter how you feel or how you interpret what's going on in your life, every tiny thing you do towards releasing your inner pain and finding self-acceptance and peace takes you a step closer to living an Ed-free life.

Keep reciting French psychologist Émile Coué's mantra: *Every day in every way I'm getting better and better.* You are!

You know you're letting go of Ed when...

You're down in the dumps, sick of battling Ed, convinced it's all a waste of effort and heartache and that you're getting nowhere. Time for a monstrous binge, you decide, to help you forget how crappy you feel for a while. Wearily, you trudge into the kitchen, open the freezer and begin rummaging for something, anything to eat. But hang on, what's that? A half-open tub of ice cream! Now how long has that been there? A week!? You mean to say some time ago you had a bowl of ice-cream, decided you'd had enough, left the rest and then forgot about it entirely? Blimey, that's a first...

Hallelujah! A glimmer of light on the horizon! These are the moments that make all the difference, that show you that quietly, gently Ed is slipping away.

Here are some other signs to look out for that show you're making progress:

- You feel happy, truly happy, for one precious moment.
- You pass a mirror without looking in it.
- You eat something, taste it, savor it, enjoy it.
- You can't be bothered to beat yourself up for doing something "wrong".
- You laugh more.
- You do something crazy, impulsive and purely for fun.
- You do something for yourself, without seeing it as selfish.
- You tell someone how you feel: happy, sad, scared, mad.
- You do something nice for your body, like touching or massaging it gently.
- You buy a chocolate advent calendar and only open one door a day.
- You break one of your Ed rules and the world doesn't end.
- You say: "I like that," or "I don't like that," "I want that,"

or "I don't want that," "I need that," or "I don't need that."

- You walk away from a negative, competitive friend.
- You forget to weigh/measure yourself one day.
- You think about a future without Ed and it feels good.
- You get very angry about something and scream/cry/shout/stamp all the rage out.
- You cry, and then you feel better.
- You screw up and think, "Oh well."
- You have more energy and more interest in the world.
- You get excited about a new activity, goal or dream.
- You make a new friend who's interested in you, not your Ed.
- You talk about Ed a little less.
- You think about Ed a little less.

Look out for little changes like these and when you notice them really celebrate each one and feel proud for your achievement. You're getting there!

Discovering life after Ed

There is so much life after Ed, so much to feel, to experience, to learn, to grab hold of, to bury yourself in, to rejoice in, to embrace. Everyone's recovery is different, but one thing is certain: life without Ed is never the same as life before Ed. After all, Ed was about changing your life, and so change is exactly what recovery brings.

For me, recovery fulfilled many of the dreams I had for myself, but it also brought plenty of surprises, taking me to places I never knew existed. Following are some of my truths about life after Ed. Perhaps these will be your truths too, or perhaps you'll experience a whole host of other fabulous ways to live.

Food:

- Food becomes fuel and a way to nurture your body.
- Sometimes, food is a way to treat yourself, and that's okay.
- Sometimes you eat "too much" and that's okay.
- Food tastes good.
- Food shopping becomes a chore (think trolley rage), but not a gut-wrenching, agonizing nightmare.
- You enjoy eating out sometimes, and order the creamy sauce rather than the tomato-based one if you fancy it.
- You stop counting calories, weighing food and keeping track of everything that passes your lips. Honest!
- You enjoy preparing food and experimenting with new flavors.
- Food becomes a pretty mundane and minor part of your life, and when someone asks you what you had for breakfast, you may well have to stop and ponder for a while.

Mind:

- You forget to notice how your behaviors and feelings change: instead of focusing on Ed, food, your body and your pain, it slips away, until one day you find yourself realizing, "Wow, it's been ages since I felt that/did that."
- You no longer need to control in the same way, which means the terror associated with losing that control dissipates.
- Feelings become less terrifying, less overwhelming, and you understand that by sitting with them and accepting them, they will pass.
- You aren't a good person if you do x, and a bad person if you do y. You're just you.
- Perfection is a pain in the butt you'd rather not strive for.

Your best does nicely instead.

- Compulsions lose their grip: where there was, "I must do this," you discover, "I can do this, if I choose."
- The vice around your mind loosens: you're free from the spinning, the pressure and the tightness.
- You screw up sometimes, and that's fine. In fact, it's quite liberating to get things wrong or to be utterly useless at something.
- Life moves from extremes to middle ground.
- You become attracted to inner rather than outer beauty in others.
- You stop thinking about Ed, and even forget what life used to be like. Sometimes you stand back and remember, and then you feel sad for the old you, and happy and proud of the new you.
- You live in the moment, rather than always looking backwards at the painful past or fretting over the uncertain future.

Body:

- Compulsive weighing/measuring goes out the window (hopefully, you smash the scales to smithereens and never buy a new set).
- You look in the mirror without freaking out and feeling overwhelmed by hate and disgust.
- You live within your body, not without: you feel pain, tiredness, tingles, caresses, gurgles.
- You touch yourself without terror.
- You nurture your body and do your best to make up for the times you abused it and hurt it.
- You abandon trying to force your body to be a certain shape and size; instead, you try to be healthy and strong.
- You appreciate how miraculous your body is: each sneeze,

each yawn, each ache, each movement.

- You accept your body's natural size, whatever that may be, and trust that your body knows best.

Soul:

- You experience times of pure joy, blissful inner peace, exhilarating excitement and tingly, warming love.
- Sometimes, you feel rubbish—sad, fatigued, angry, ashamed, aching—and that's okay. It's all part of life.
- It's good to be alive. You want to be alive. You treasure life and all the feelings it brings.
- Hope carries you. You've been to the darkest place inside and come back. Nothing can extinguish that flame now.
- You have faith: in the world, in people, in your loved ones and most of all in yourself.
- You feel guided, protected by the universe, that you're safe and always will be.
- You feel at peace.

Looking back without regret

Finally, I want to share with you the best kept secret of recovery: *I don't regret my eating disorder.*

You're probably wondering how I can say this. Don't I look back over years of misery, pain and terrible self-abuse and regret it all? The answer is no. I regret the fact that I *needed* to have eating disorder, but I don't regret *having* an eating disorder. Let me explain...

I look back over my past and I feel sad that it had to be that way for me. I feel sad for the little girl who got abused, and for the young woman who was in so much pain she abused herself. I feel sad that I needed to live through the horrors of an eating disorder, and that those around me were hurt by my illness as well. I feel sad that my life took me to a point where I could see no way out, no way to survive, without Ed.

But I don't beat myself up for befriending Ed. I was in terrible pain and I couldn't cope. I needed Ed to help me survive. And Ed got me through some very tough times, until I was ready to deal with my pain and let go.

If I hadn't got an eating disorder, I wouldn't be where I am today. The severity of Ed's impact on my life forced me to face the feelings I had buried within, but without Ed I may have just kept carrying the pain inside forever, and been quietly but completely miserable.

The work I did in recovering from Ed has made me the woman I am now, a woman I'm proud to be. Thanks to Ed and the healing journey I went on to let it go, I'm now happy, well, connected to the world, and writing a book about eating disorder recovery.

And there's something very liberating about having been so far down in life and then got back up again. Whatever life throws at me now, I know I'll be okay. And strange as it sounds, the very possibility that I could ever relapse keeps me always making the right choices for me, so that I could never get ill again. Having Ed in the first place, and then letting it go, has been become one of the defining elements of who I am and where I'm going in life. And I'm grateful for that.

Forgiving yourself for having your eating disorder releases you from all the guilt, the blame, the self-hate. It's okay that you got an eating disorder; you needed it. What counts is what you do with your eating disorder: whether you spend your life in its grip, running from yourself, or whether you recover and experience all the great things life has to offer. You can't change the past, but you can change the future. As Robbie Williams so eloquently put it:

No regrets; they don't work.

No regrets; they only hurt.

Afterword

Thirty years ago, one cold December evening, my mother kissed goodnight her newborn baby, never suspecting that would be their last moment together, never knowing that a new chapter was about to open in her tiny daughter's life, one of loss and loneliness.

Thirty years later, the wheel came full circle. After so many years of searching and longing and grieving, I discovered a mother's love at last in the reflection of my newborn baby's eyes.

Because as this book grew, so did I. The body I'd once thought was ugly and weak and useless blossomed into a cocoon for a dancing, wiggling, kicking little person. And I discovered a strength I never thought existed within me the day I brought my son into the world.

I felt happy, at peace, complete. But just months later I found myself standing on the edge of an abyss, looking down.

My son, my gorgeous George, fell suddenly and gravely ill with a brain infection. All I had ever wanted for my child was that he would grow up safe in my love, untouched by the kind of pain and fear I'd known as a child. And now my baby was in agony and terrified, and I couldn't make it all better for him. I stood by, desperate and helpless, as neurosurgeons operated on his brain. And then I spent many weeks living with him in a London hospital ward while drugs battled his infection.

Within a few days of his surgery, George was fine in himself again: smiling, laughing, cuddling. And I smiled and laughed and cuddled him back, but inside it felt like something was breaking.

There was no time or space for me to deal with the feelings that kept threatening to overwhelm me: the terror, the shock, the sadness, the anger. I was miles from home, I was getting very little sleep and I was living on snack food from the hospital shop.

Unsurprisingly, it wasn't long before Ed began tapping on my shoulder with promises to be there for me, to support me, to make the feelings less painful, to make the experience less terrible, to give me control in a world of chaos.

This was the biggest test to my recovery I'd encountered, and at first I was terrified. But as I sat with my fear, it melted away and was replaced with a sense of calm. I was aware of Ed's voice, but somehow it didn't interest me. I didn't need to struggle with myself and battle not to give into Ed. Instead, I felt a lovely, gentle voice inside reassure me that everything would be okay, that it was alright to feel rather than run from my feelings, and that I didn't deserve to hurt myself over my son being hurt. I knew then that I didn't need Ed to help me through this. I could do it myself.

And I did. My son healed, and I healed, and life, happily, went on.

And Ed remained nothing more than a memory on the pages of this book.

About the author

Pippa Wilson is a writer and book editor. She lives in Kent, England, with her husband and son.

You can find out more on her website, www.eatingdisorders-recovery.com

BOOKS

O is a symbol of the world, of oneness and unity. In different cultures it also means the "eye," symbolizing knowledge and insight. We aim to publish books that are accessible, constructive and that challenge accepted opinion, both that of academia and the "moral majority."

Our books are available in all good English language bookstores worldwide. If you don't see the book on the shelves ask the bookstore to order it for you, quoting the ISBN number and title. Alternatively you can order online (all major online retail sites carry our titles) or contact the distributor in the relevant country, listed on the copyright page.

See our website **www.o-books.net** for a full list of over 500 titles, growing by 100 a year.

And tune in to myspiritradio.com for our book review radio show, hosted by June-Elleni Laine, where you can listen to the authors discussing their books.

MySpiritRadio